KU-619-830

BrightRED Results

Standard Grade
FRENCH

Emma-Jane Welsh

First published in 2009 by:
Bright Red Publishing Ltd
6 Stafford Street
Edinburgh
EH3 7AU

Copyright © Bright Red Publishing Ltd 2009

Cover image © Caleb Rutherford

All rights reserved. No part of this publication may be reproduced, stored in a retrieval system, or transmitted in any form or by any means, electronic, mechanical, photocopying, recording or otherwise, without prior permission in writing from the publisher.

The right of Emma-Jane Welsh to be identified as the author of this work has been asserted by her in accordance with sections 77 and 78 of the Copyright, Designs and Patents Act 1988

A CIP record for this book is available from the British Library

ISBN 978-1-906736-25-5

With thanks to:
Pumpkin House, Cambridge (layout), Angela Clare and Alex Hepworth (editorial)

Cover design by Caleb Rutherford – e i d e t i c

Illustrations by Pumpkin House, Cambridge

Every effort has been made to seek all copyright holders. If any have been overlooked then Bright Red Publishing will be delighted to make the necessary arrangements.

Bright Red Publishing would like to make the following acknowledgement for permission to reproduce extracts within this text: "Sound of the Underground", p.32, words and music by Brian Thomas Higgins, Niara Scarlett and Miranda Eleanor de Fonbrune Cooper © Xenomania Music (NS) and Warner/Chappell Music Ltd (PRS). All rights administered by WB Music Corp.

Bright Red Publishing would like to thank the Scottish Qualifications Authority for use of Past Exam questions. Answers do not emanate from SQA.

Printed and bound in Scotland by Scotprint

Contents

What does Standard Grade French involve?

Standard Grade French is a two-year course spread over Third and Fourth Year of your Secondary schooling, and results in a Credit, General or a Foundation award. What really matters about *Standard Grade French* is the course itself:

▶ the vocabulary

▶ the language skills.

You will need to know vocabulary from all of the topics studied in First and Second Year, ranging from school subjects and pets to ordering food in a restaurant and giving directions. You will also need to be competent in five main tenses: the present, the future, the conditional and two past tenses (the perfect and imperfect). It is helpful also to be familiar with the imperative tense. You will need to be able to recognise these tenses (visually in reading passages and aurally in listening extracts) to understand the time period they refer to and to use them when writing essays on a range of Standard Grade topics.

Your *Standard Grade French* course is also about developing the key skills of Reading, Listening, Writing and Speaking. As you improve in one of these skills, the others will automatically improve. For example, as your reading of texts develops, you can use the vocabulary you learn in your writing and speaking. You will also be able to pick out the same words in the Listening paper. As you develop your skills as a listener, your pronunciation and vocabulary will improve. This will help your speaking skills and, in turn, further develop your comprehension of listening extracts. Each skill that you practise in French will develop your overall competence in the language.

The skills that you develop during your Standard Grade course will be assessed in three ways.

1 A Folio of coursework, assessed externally.

2 An external examination in Reading and Listening.

3 An internal assessment of Speaking.

In Standard Grade, the word 'assessment' refers to the work that you complete in class and at home, and the word 'examination' refers to the tests you sit in May in the examination hall.

How your Standard Grade French course is assessed

The Folio

Your Folio of coursework must be submitted to the Scottish Qualifications Authority (SQA) by 31 March on the year of the examination. It includes three essays on different Standard Grade topics, for example holidays, health or school. The three essays must be about 150 words each in length and:

▶ recount personal experience

▶ provide information

▶ express ideas

▶ express opinions and preferences

▶ give reasons.

The exam

The external examination takes place in May and is made up of two Reading papers and two Listening papers. The two Reading papers will be a General paper (45 minutes) which assesses Grades 4 and 3, and *either*:

▶ a Credit paper (1 hour) which assesses Grades 2 and 1, *or*

▶ a Foundation paper (45 minutes) which assesses Grades 5 and 6.

Candidates must read the text in French and answer five or six questions in English on a variety of topics. The use of a dictionary is permitted and recommended. The two Listening papers will be a General paper (25 minutes) and a Credit paper (30 minutes).

Look out for

Make sure that you check the level of your paper as soon as you sit down in the exam room. For example, if you are sitting Credit, you should not have a Foundation paper in front of you. If the paper seems too easy or too difficult, you could be sitting the wrong paper!

Look out for

The Reading paper is double weighted, which means that the grade you achieve will be twice as important as your grade for the Listening paper. Although the Listening paper is worth the least, it is statistically the hardest to pass, so you must practise listening to spoken French as much as possible and revise your vocabulary thoroughly. You must prepare thoroughly for all the elements of your Standard Grade.

The Speaking assessment

Your skill in Speaking is assessed internally by your teacher. During class, you will complete several speaking tests which fall into the categories of presentation, discussion and role-play. The presentation involves your speaking for one to two minutes on a prepared topic. The topic may be the same as one of your Folio pieces. During this assessment, you will be allowed to have three headings in front of you, with a maximum of three words each in either French or English. For the discussion, you need to have a conversation for three to five minutes on an agreed topic with either the teacher or another student. The role-play will also last about three to five minutes and will be about exchanging information to offer or request services, for example in a clothes shop or a tourist office. Like the discussion, the role-play can be carried out with the teacher or another student. If you wish, you may choose to carry out your Speaking assessments with only your teacher present. The best marks for each of these three exercises will be the basis of your final Speaking grade. Like the Reading paper, the grades for Speaking are double weighted.

Grade Related Criteria

Grade Related Criteria (GRC) are the criteria used by the SQA markers to mark your Folio and/or your external examinations (Reading and Listening). Each marker will use the relevant set of GRC when setting your tasks and marking the work you do throughout the course. The GRC can be found on the SQA website, at www.sqa.org.uk/sqa.files_ccc/miModLangSGFolioWritingEARLY.pdf.

How does the SQA arrive at your final grade?

Once your Folio has been externally assessed and your Reading and Listening papers marked, your overall mark is calculated as follows:

▶ Writing: single weighted (1)

▶ Reading: double weighted (2)

▶ Listening: single weighted (1)

▶ Speaking: double weighted (2)

The marks you achieve for your Reading and Speaking are doubled and the marks for Writing and Listening are added up normally. The total is then divided by 6.

Imagine, for example, that you achieved these grades: Writing 2, Reading 2, Listening 3, Speaking 1. This would be calculated as 2 + 2 (+ 2) + 3 + 1 (+ 1) = 11. The total of 11 divided by 6 gives 1.8 Your overall grade would therefore be a 2.

How this book can help you

Although *Standard Grade French* is a two-year course, **BrightRED Results:** *Standard Grade French* focuses on your work in the year leading up to the examination (usually your Fourth year at school). It offers you a study 'toolkit' containing:

▶ essential language rules and vocabulary

▶ suggestions to help you improve your skills

▶ effective techniques for handling exam questions

▶ a range of typical types of questions from Past Papers

▶ a range of ways to revise, either on your own or with friends.

Writing essays

Chapter 5 The Folio (Writing) explains how to structure your essays in French and includes a model essay. You are advised to choose a topic which enables you to 'show off' your knowledge of a variety of tenses and to redraft your work so that you can express yourself in a variety of sentence constructions and vocabulary. Chapter 1 Language skills will be an essential resource for you as it contains grammatical information on types of sentences and six tenses. It includes verb tables showing you how to form the most essential regular and irregular verbs. Common grammatical terms are highlighted in the book.

Reading comprehension

Chapter 3 The Reading paper gives you an analysis of the types of questions which have been used in previous General and Credit Reading exams. For each type of question, a technique is offered to help you approach it in an effective way. You will learn how to find key information quickly in the French passage and to write the quantity and quality of answers that will get full marks. For each type of question, examples are provided from Past Papers. The first of these is worked through with you and there is always at least one extra question for you to try on your own. The answers for these 'self-test' questions are provided at the end of the book. Since you are allowed a dictionary in the Reading paper, Chapter 2 Dictionary skills shows you how to get the most out of your French–English English–French dictionary under the stressful conditions of an exam.

Aural comprehension

Chapter 7 Vocabulary offers you a comprehensive list of topic vocabulary. If you learn all these words and phrases, and can recognise them visually and aurally, you will greatly improve your grades. Learning vocabulary will stand you in good stead for all your exams, but it is especially important preparation for the Listening exam, as use of a dictionary is not permitted. Chapter 4 The Listening paper suggests a range of ways to memorise vocabulary, some of which give full rein to your creativity! Like Chapter 3 The Reading paper, Chapter 4 offers you an analysis of types of questions from Past Papers, and works through examples of each type, giving you effective techniques. You will learn how to approach the questions more actively, pick out key words from the recording, identify the correct answers and gain the maximum marks you can. Audio files are available free for the Listening questions online at www.brightredpublishing.co.uk/ and transcripts for the audio files can be found at the back of the book. Only refer to the transcripts after you have attempted the questions by listening to the audio files. Answers for the self-test questions are at the end of the book.

Speaking

Chapter 6 The Speaking assessment helps you to prepare for the presentation, discussion and role-play assessments. Many students find that the work they have done for their Folio is good preparation for this but that it needs to be adjusted to sound more natural and spontaneous. The websites listed in Chapter 4 The Listening paper will be a good resource to help 'tune your French ear' and improve your pronunciation. Similarly, Chapter 4 also lists pronunciation points you should be aware of. Chapter 5 The Folio (Writing) gives guidance on ways to memorise your work.

Beyond the exam

Not only will this book help you to prepare for and do well in *Standard Grade French*, it will also help lay down the skills you need next year to do well in *Higher French* and the Baccalaureate exam, if you go down that route.

Using Past Papers

To revise effectively for your *Standard Grade French* exam, it is useful to complete Past Paper questions in Reading and Listening. As mentioned above, Chapters 3 and 4 of this book establish a good method for dealing with each question type. However, try to test yourself further on other Past Paper questions. These are published every year (currently by Bright Red Publishing) and make good revision practice.

The Reading paper questions are straightforward as you have the information you need to hand. However, completing the Listening papers is more problematic if you only have a copy of the transcript. Remember, though, that you can download the audio files from www.brightredpublishing.co.uk at no charge. You should not read the transcript and then complete the questions as it completely defeats the purpose of listening practice.

Rather than completing the entire Listening or Reading paper and then correcting it using the answers at the back, it is more useful to check the answers after each question while the text is fresh in your mind. This way, you will gain a better understanding of where you went wrong and it may prevent you from making similar mistakes in the next question.

Another way to study using Past Papers is to concentrate on one type of question at a time. Chapters 3 and 4 of this book offer techniques to help you complete each type of question. Use these guidelines and go through every year completing the same types of questions, particularly the ones you find most difficult. By the end of this exercise, you will be an expert on every type of question!

Every aspect of General and Credit *Standard Grade French* demands well-developed language skills. You have to be able to:

▶ recognise different parts of speech in the Reading paper so that you can look up words in the dictionary and can translate sentences into the correct tense

▶ recognise different parts of speech and tenses aurally in the Listening paper

▶ use a variety of tenses in your Writing Folio and in your Speaking assessments.

Your skill in these areas depends upon your understanding of the grammatical rules underpinning the language. A good knowledge of French grammar will increase your marks in the Reading and Listening, allow you to write excellent Folio and Speaking pieces, and also give you a firm grounding in the French language, enabling you to tackle every part of the *Standard Grade French* course with ease.

Different types of sentences

There are three kinds of sentences that you should be aware of:

▶ simple

▶ compound

▶ complex.

Simple sentences

The most basic kind of sentence is the **simple sentence**. It has only one main verb. For example:

Paul joue au foot. Paul plays football.

The **verb** is traditionally defined as 'the doing word' and describes an action. There are also verbs of 'being' such as 'to have' and 'to be'. You can put 'to' before a verb in the **infinitive** (full) form. For example, you can say 'to be' but you cannot say 'to is'. Similarly, you can say 'to play' but you cannot say 'to plays'.

In the example, the verb is quite definitely the 'doing' word. What does Paul do? He plays football! To confirm that 'play' is the verb, you can put 'to' before 'play' (the infinitive form).

Compound sentences

Compound sentences are two simple sentences which are joined together with the **conjunctions** *et* (and) or *ou* (or). They therefore contain two verbs of equal importance, for example:

Paul joue au foot et Sarah fait du judo. Paul plays football and Sarah does Judo.

Either half of the sentence can be taken away and the other half will still make sense.

Complex sentences

Complex sentences contain one main verb and a subordinate verb, introduced by the conjuction, *qui* (who). For example:

Paul, qui a douze ans joue au foot. Paul, who is 12 years old, plays football.

Look out for

To achieve Credit grades in your Folio pieces it is essential that you use complex sentences, so make sure you understand how to use them.

This sentence has a **main clause** (*Paul joue au foot*) and a **subordinate clause** (*qui a douze ans*). The sentence will make sense without the subordinate clause, but not without the main clause. Within the subordinate clause, the subordinate verb is *a* (has). This time the verb is not a verb of action, but you can say 'to have' which confirms that it is a verb.

Articles

In English there is only one word for the **articles** 'the', 'some' and 'a' (or 'an'), but in French there are several words for these because they agree with nouns in **gender** and **number**.

	Masculine	Feminine	Plural
the	*le (l')*	*la (l')*	*les*
a / an	*un*	*une*	*des*
some	*du (de l')*	*de la (de l')*	*des*

J'ai bu un café. I drank a coffee.
J'ai bu le café. I drank the coffee.
J'ai bu du café. I drank some coffee.

Il y a une araignée noire. There is a black spider.
Il y a l'araignée noire. There is the black spider.
Il y a des araignées noires. There are black spiders.

Possessive adjectives

Possessive adjectives are the words for 'my', 'your', 'his', 'her', 'our' and 'their'. They agree in gender and number with the nouns they describe.

	Singular		Plural
	Masculine	**Feminine**	
my	mon	ma	mes
your	ton	ta	tes
his/her	son	sa	ses
our	notre	notre	nos
your	votre	votre	vos
their	leur	leur	leurs

C'est mon père. It is my father. (masc.: *le père*)

C'est ma mere. It is my mother. (fem.: *la mère*)

Ce sont mes parents. It is my parents. (pl.: *les parents*)

Faîtes votre travail! Do your work! (masc.: *le travail*)

Faîtes votre valise! Pack your suitcase! (fem.: *la valise*)

Faîtes vos devoirs! Do your homework! (pl.: *les devoirs*)

Adjectives

When it comes to the position of adjectives in a sentence, the word order in French is usually different to that in English. For example, while we would say 'a brown dog', the French would say *un chien marron* (a dog brown). Remember this when you are translating sentences in the Reading paper otherwise your answers will not make sense! Adjectives usually come after the noun and always agree in gender and number with the nouns they are describing.

Singular		Plural	
Masculine	**Feminine**	**Masculine**	**Feminine**
Basic adjective from dictionary.	Add extra –e, but words ending in: –e do not change –eux change to –euse –er change to –ère –f change to –ve –c change to –che.	Add an –s, but words ending in: –eux do not change.	Add an –es, but words ending in: –e just take an –s –eux cahnge to –eures –er change to –ères –f change to –ves. –c change to –ches.
grand	*grande*	*grands*	*grandes*
rose	*rose*	*roses*	*roses*
paresseux	*paresseuse*	*paresseux*	*paresseuses*
premier	*première*	*premiers*	*premières*
éducatif	*éducative*	*éducatifs*	*éducatives*
blanc	*blanche*	*blancs*	*blanches*

Verb tenses

The tense of a verb allows us to express events in time. You need to know the different tenses to write your Folio pieces, to perform well in your Speaking and to understand Reading and Listening passages. Although there are lots of tenses in French, we are going to concentrate on six of the most important ones: the **present tense**, the **imperfect tense**, the **perfect tense**, the **imperative tense**, the **future tense** and the **conditional**.

There are three types of verbs in French: verbs ending in –er (for example, *regarder* 'to look'), verbs ending –ir (for example, *finir* 'to finish') and verbs ending in –re (for example, *vendre* 'to sell'). Each of these three types of verbs form the above six tenses differently.

The present tense

To form the present tense of verbs, you take off the ending of the –er, –ir or –re verb. This leaves you with the **stem**. For example the stem of *regarder* is *regard*. For each group of verbs, you then add the endings shown below to the stem.

–er verbs, for example *regarder* to watch

Present tense formation of *regarder* to watch		
Pronoun	**Ending**	**Example**
je (I)	–e	regard**e**
tu (you, sing.)	–es	regard**es**
il/elle (he/she)	–e	regard**e**
nous (we)	–ons	regard**ons**
vous (you, pl.)	–ez	regard**ez**
ils (they, masc.)/ *elles* (they, fem.)	–ent	regard**ent**

If you wanted to say 'I watch', you would say *je regarde* and if you wanted to say 'we watch', you would say *nous regardons*.

–ir verbs, for example *finir* to finish

Present tense formation of *finir* to finish		
Pronoun	**Ending**	**Example**
je (I)	–is	fin**is**
tu (you, sing.)	–is	fin**is**
il/elle (he/she)	–it	fin**it**
nous (we)	–issons	fin**issons**
vous (you, pl.)	–issez	fin**issez**
ils (they, masc.)/ *elles* (they, fem.)	–issent	fin**issent**

If you wanted to say 'I finish', you would say *je finis* and if you wanted to say 'we finish', you would say *nous finissons*.

Some –ir verbs are **irregular** and take the –er ending in the present tense, for example *ouvrir* (to open).

ouvrir to open	
j'ouvre	*nous ouvrons*
tu ouvres	*vous ouvrez*
il/elle ouvre	*ils/elles ouvrent*

Another group of *–ir* verbs, for example *dormir* (to sleep) and *partir* (to leave) lose the last **consonant** of their stem in the present and take these endings: *–s, –s, –t, –ons, –ez, –ent*.

partir to leave	
je pars	*nous partons*
tu pars	*vous partez*
il/elle part	*ils/elles partent*

Look out for

Of the irregular *–ir* verbs, *ouvrir*, *dormir* and *partir* are the most important verbs to learn.

–re verbs, for example *vendre* to sell

Present tense formation of *vendre* to sell		
Pronoun	**Ending**	**Example**
je (I)	*–s*	vend**s**
tu (you, sing.)	*–s*	vend**s**
il/elle (he/she)	–	vend
nous (we)	*–ons*	vend**ons**
vous (you, pl.)	*–ez*	vend**ez**
ils (they, masc.)/ *elles* (they, fem.)	*–ent*	vend**ent**

If you wanted to say 'I sell', you would say *je vends* and if you wanted to say 'we sell', you would say *nous vendons*.

These rules apply to **regular verbs** in the present tense but there are also many irregular verbs which follow a different pattern altogether. There is no alternative but to learn irregular verbs off by heart.

Irregular verbs

The two most common irregular verbs are *avoir* (to have) and *être* (to be). Not only do you need these to write in the present tense, but they are also essential when you come to form the perfect tense. They are **conjugated** as follows:

avoir to have	
j'ai I have	*nous avons* we have
tu as you have	*vous avez* you have
il/elle a he/she has	*ils/elles ont* they have

être to be	
je suis I am	*nous sommes* we are
tu es you are	*vous êtes* you are
il/elle est he/she is	*ils/elles sont* they are

You will also need to recognise and use the following verbs:

aller to go	
je vais I go	*nous allons* we go
tu vas you go	*vous allez* you go
il/elle va he/she goes	*ils/elles vont* they go

faire to do	
je fais I do	*nous faisons* we do
tu fais you do	*vous faites* you do
il/elle fait he/she does	*ils/elles font* they do

voir to see	
je vois I see	*nous voyons* we see
tu vois you see	*vous voyez* you see
il/elle voit he/she sees	*ils/elles voient* they see

boire to drink	
je bois I drink	*nous buvons* we drink
tu bois you drink	*vous buvez* you drink
il/elle boit he/she drinks	*ils/elles boivent* they drink

pouvoir to be able to	
je peux I can	*nous pouvons* we can
tu peux you can	*vous pouvez* you can
il/elle peut he/she can	*ils/elles peuvent* they can

savoir to know	
je sais I know	*nous savons* we know
tu sais you know	*vous savez* you know
il/elle sait he/she knows	*ils/elles savent* they know

recevoir to receive	
je reçois I receive	*nous recevons* we receive
tu reçois you receive	*vous recevez* you receive
il/elle reçoit he/she receives	*ils/elles reçoivent* they receive

devoir to have to	
je dois I must	*nous devons* we must
tu dois you must	*vous devez* you must
il/elle doit he/she must	*ils/elles doivent* they must

Reflexive verbs

Reflexive verbs are used to talk about things that one does to oneself. For example, when talking about your daily routine you might say *je me lave* (I wash myself). Reflexive verbs follow the normal patterns of present tense –*er*, –*ir* or –*re* verbs but have an extra word between the **subject** (*je, tu, il/elle* …) and the verb (*lave, couche,* …) which is called a **reflexive pronoun** (*me, te, se, nous, vous, se*).

Reflexive pronouns	
me/m' myself	*nous* ourselves
te/t' yourself	*vous* yourselves
se/s' himself/herself	*se/s'* themselves

The following example shows how to form reflexive verbs. The verb *se laver* means 'to wash oneself' or 'to get washed'. It is a regular –*er* verb so you conjugate it as usual by taking off the –*er* ending and adding the endings –*e, –es, –e, –ons, –ez* and –*ent*.

je lave I wash   *nous lavons* we wash

tu laves you wash   *vous lavez* you wash

il/elle lave he/she washes   *ils/elles lavent* they wash

However, this means 'I wash', not 'I wash myself' or 'I get washed'. You still need to add in the reflexive pronoun between the subject and the verb as shown in the table.

se laver to wash oneself/get washed	
je **me** *lave* I wash myself	*nous* **nous** *lavons* we wash ourselves
tu **te** *laves* you wash yourself	*vous* **vous** *lavez* you wash yourselves
il/elles **se** *lave* he/she washes himself/herself	*ils/elles* **se** *lavent* they wash themselves

Some common reflexive verbs:

s'appeler   to be called*

se coucher   to go to bed

se doucher   to have a shower

s'habiller   to get dressed

s'inscrire   to sign up/apply*

se lever   to get up*

se rendre compte   to realise

se réveiller   to wake up

*Irregular verbs

The imperfect tense

You use the imperfect tense when you want to talk about something that you:

▶ did several times in the past

▶ used to do

▶ were doing when you were interrupted by something else.

It is often translated in English by 'was …–ing ', for example 'I was eating' (when the doorbell rang).

1 *Je mangeais un hamburger quand il est venu*. I was eating a hamburger when he came. (Interrupted action)

2 *Tous les jours, j'allais aux magasins*. Every day I went to the shops. (Repeated action in the past)

3 *Quand j'étais enfant, je buvais du lait*. When I was a child, I drank milk. (Something you used to do)

To form the imperfect tense, you take the stem of the *nous* part of the present tense (for example, *nous regardons*, take off *–ons*, so the stem is *regard–*) and add the endings shown below.

Imperfect tense formation of *regarder* to watch		
Pronoun	Ending	Example
je (I)	*–ais*	*regardais*
tu (you, sing.)	*–ais*	*regardais*
il/elle (he/she)	*–ait*	*regardait*
nous (we)	*–ions*	*regardions*
vous (you, pl.)	*–iez*	*regardiez*
ils (they, masc.)/*elles* (they, fem.)	*–aient*	*regardaient*

The only exception to this rule is the verb *être* which is conjugated as follows:

être to be	
j'étais I was	*nous étions* we were
tu étais you were	*vous étiez* you were
il/elle était he/she was	*ils/elles étaient* they were

It is tempting just to take the usual stem of the verb to form the imperfect but this does not work with every verb so always use the *nous* stem.

The perfect tense

The perfect tense is one of the most commonly used of all tenses. It is used to describe completed actions in the past and it is often followed by a precise time or date.

1 *L'année dernière je suis allé(e) à Paris.* Last year I went to Paris. (Specific time)

2 *Hier, j'ai fait mes devoirs.* Yesterday, I did my homework.

3 *Il y a deux mois, j'ai joué au badminton avec mon copain.* Two months ago, I played badminton with my friend.

To form the perfect tense you need two components:

(1) **auxiliary verb** + (2) **past participle**.

1 Auxiliary verb: this is the present tense of *avoir*, or in some cases *être* – both of which you know already!

avoir to have	
j'ai I have	*nous avons* we have
tu as you have	*vous avez* you have
il/elle a he/she has	*ils/elles ont* they have

être to be	
je suis I am	*nous sommes* we are
tu es you are	*vous êtes* you are
il/elle est he/she is	*ils/elles sont* they are

2

Forming the past participle		
–er verbs	*–ir* verbs	*–re* verbs
take off the *–er* ending and add *–é*	take off the *–ir* ending and add *–i*	take off the *–re* ending and add *–u*

continued

If you want to say 'I bought a jumper', you would:

1 Take the auxiliary verb *avoir* and get *j'ai*.

2 Form the past participle of *acheter* (take off the *–er* and add *–é*).

3 Find the word for 'jumper' (*un pull*) and then join it together.

4 This gives: *J'ai acheté un pull.*

How would you say 'He sold a book?' Do the same thing: use the auxiliary verb *avoir* and get *il a*, then form the past participle of *vendre* (take off the *–re* and add *–u*), find the word for 'book' (*un livre*) and then join it all together to get: *Il a vendu un livre.*

The perfect tense – continued

There are quite a few irregular verbs in the perfect tense. Here are the most common ones that you should learn.

Irregular verbs in the perfect tense			
Verb	**Meaning**	**Past participle**	**Meaning**
apprendre	to learn	*appris*	learned
faire	to do, to make	*fait*	did, made
recevoir	to receive	*reçu*	received
construire	to build	*construit*	built
boire	to drink	*bu*	drank
découvrir	to discover	*découvert*	discovered
produire	to produce	*produit*	produced
écrire	to write	*écrit*	wrote

To form expressions with these verbs you do the same as for regular verbs (that is, you find the auxiliary verb) but instead of taking off the ending from the main verb, you just use the irregular past participle from the table above. For example, to say 'we discovered' you would say *nous avons découvert*.

All of the examples given above use *avoir* as the auxiliary verb and this is the case for most verbs. However, the verbs in the next table use *être* as the auxiliary.

continued

The perfect tense – continued

Verbs which form the perfect tense with *être*		
Verb	**Meaning**	**Past participle**
aller (irregular)	to go	*allé* (irregular)
rester	to stay	*resté*
arriver	to arrive	*arrivé*
partir	to leave	*parti*
entrer	to enter	*entré*
sortir	to go out	*sorti*
monter	to go up	*monté*
descendre	to go down	*descendu*
*naître**	to be born	*né* (irregular)
*mourir**	to die	*mort* (irregular)
tomber	to fall	*tombé*
*venir**	to come	*venu* (irregular)
*devenir**	to become	*devenu* (irregular)
rentrer	to return	*rentré*
retourner	to return	*retourné*
*revenir**	to return	*revenu* (irregular)

*Irregular verbs (See table above for past participles)

continued

The perfect tense – continued

To help you remember them, the verbs in the table have been grouped into contrasting pairs. Another way to remember them is to use the following mnemonic:

venir + TRAMPS DEMAND 3 returns

      venir +

Tomber	*Descendre*
Rester	*Entrer*
Aller	*Mourir*
Monter	*Arriver*
Partir	*Naître*
Sortir	*Devenir*

3 returns: *rentrer, retourner, revenir*

You might have fun inventing a mnemonic of your own to help you remember these verbs.

Unlike perfect tense verbs which have *avoir* as their auxiliary, the past participles of *être* verbs have to agree in gender and number with the person doing the action. For example:

Je suis allé …	I went … (the speaker is a boy)
Je suis allée …	I went … (the speaker is a girl)
Nous sommes allés …	We went … (the speakers are two or more boys, or a group of boys and girls)
Nous sommes allées …	We went … (the speakers are two or more girls)

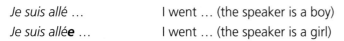

Look out for

Where there is a mix of sexes, that is a girl and a boy, or several girls and a boy, then the past participle always takes the masculine ending, for example: *nous sommes allés* (without the extra –e).

continued

How would you say 'they arrived' if you were talking about two girls?

1   Take the auxiliary verb *être* (*elles sont*).

2   Form the past participle (take off the –er and add –é) to get *arrivé*.

3   Add an extra –e (because it's feminine) and add an extra –s (because it's plural).

4   This gives: *Elles sont arrivées*.

Try this process for 'I went home'. Your verb is *rentrer*. The auxiliary verb *être* would give *je suis*, and the past participle would be *rentré*. What do you have to add onto it this time? An extra –e if the person who is speaking is female, otherwise nothing at all as this time. 'I' is only one person so you do not need to add an –s: *Je suis rentré(e)*.

The perfect tense – continued

Reflexive verbs (see page 20) also form the perfect tense with *être*.

se laver to wash oneself/get washed	
je me suis lavé(e) I washed myself	*nous nous sommes lavé(e)s* we washed ourselves
tu t'es lavé(e) you washed yourself	*vous vous êtes lavé(e)s* you washed yourselves
il/elle s'est lavé(e) he/she washed himself/ herself	*ils/elles se sont lavé(e)s* they washed themselves

The imperative tense

The imperative tense is used to give instructions, to give orders or to make suggestions and is usually followed by an exclamation mark.

Sois content! Be happy!

Regardez le tableau! Look at the painting!

Restons tranquilles! Let's take it easy!

Notice that the pronoun (*tu, nous,* or *vous*) is not actually used but is implied.

There are three forms of the imperative:

1 Second person singular (*tu* form): used when you are giving an instruction to one person.

2 Second person plural (*vous* form): used when you are giving the instruction to more than one person.

3 First person plural (*nous* form): used when you would say 'Let's …' in English and you are speaking about yourself and at least one other person.

–er verbs, for example *donner* to give

To form these verbs, you take off the –*er* ending and add the endings in the table.

Imperative of *donner* to give		
	Ending	**Example**
Second person singular (*tu*)	–e	*Donne!*
First person plural (*nous*)	–ons	*Donnons!*
Second person plural (*vous*)	–ez	*Donnez!*

–*ir* verbs, for example *finir* to finish

To form these verbs, you take off the –*ir* ending and add the endings in the table.

Imperative of *finir* to finish		
	Ending	**Example**
Second person singular *(tu)*	–*is*	*Finis!*
First person plural *(nous)*	–*issons*	*Finissons!*
Second person plural *(vous)*	–*issez*	*Finissez!*

–*re* verbs, for example *vendre* to sell

To form these verbs, you take off the –*re* ending and add the endings in the table.

Imperative of *vendre* to sell		
	Ending	**Example**
Second person singular *(tu)*	–*s*	*Vends!*
First person plural *(nous)*	–*ons*	*Vendons!*
Second person plural *(vous)*	–*ez*	*Vendez!*

Irregular verbs

However, there are some irregular forms in the imperative. Here is a list of the most important ones.

Irregular verbs in the imperative				
Verb	**Meaning**	**Second person singular** *(tu)*	**First person plural** *(nous)*	**Second person plural** *(vous)*
avoir	to have	*aie*	*ayons*	*ayez*
être	to be	*sois*	*soyons*	*soyez*
savoir	to know	*sache*	*sachons*	*sachez*
vouloir	to want	*veuille*	*	*veuillez*

*The *nous* form of *vouloir* no longer exists in the imperative tense.

The future tense

The future tense is used to express an action or event in future time, or to express probability.

1 *Je te donnerai le livre demain*. I'll give you the book tomorrow. (Action in the future)

2 *Ce sera ton frère à la porte*. That'll be your brother at the door. (Probability)

Forming *–er* and *–ir* verbs in the future tense

To form the future of both *–er* and *–ir* verbs you use the infinitive (the full form of the verb) + the following endings:

Future tense formation of *regarder* to watch, *finir* to finish		
Pronoun	**Ending**	**Example**
je (I)	*–ai*	*regarderai, finirai*
tu (you, sing.)	*–as*	*regarderas, finiras*
il/elle (he/she)	*–a*	*regardera, finira*
nous (we)	*–ons*	*regarderons, finirons*
vous (you, pl.)	*–ez*	*regarderez, finirez*
ils (they, masc.)/ *elles* (they, fem.)	*–ont*	*regarderont, finiront*

Forming *–re* verbs in the future tense

The *–re* verbs follow the same pattern but first they drop the final *–e* off the infinitive, (*vendre* ▸ *vendr–*) as follows:

Future tense formation of *vendre* to sell		
Pronoun	**Ending**	**Example**
je (I)	*–ai*	*vendrai*
tu (you, sing.)	*–as*	*vendras*
il/elle (he/she)	*–a*	*vendra*
nous (we)	*–ons*	*vendrons*
vous (you, pl.)	*–ez*	*vendrez*
ils (they, masc.)/ *elles* (they, fem.)	*–ont*	*vendront*

Irregular verbs in the future tense

The following verbs are irregular in the *je* form of the verb. The other parts of the verb (*tu, il/elle, nous, vous, ils/elles*) are formed using the same endings as regular future tense verbs, for example *tu devras* (you will have to).

Verb	Future tense	Meaning
aller	*j'irai*	I will go
avoir	*j'aurai*	I will have
courir	*je courrai*	I will run
devoir	*je devrai*	I will have to
être	*je serai*	I will be
faire	*je ferai*	I will do/make
pouvoir	*je pourrai*	I will be able to
recevoir	*je recevrai*	I will receive
savoir	*je saurai*	I will know
venir	*je viendrai*	I will come
voir	*je verrai*	I will see
vouloir	*je voudrai*	I will want

The conditional tense

The conditional tense is used when you are being hypothetical and want to say what you 'would' do.

1   *Je voudrais aller à l'université.* I **would** like to go to university.

2   *Il vendrait sa voiture pour pouvoir plus voyager!* He **would** sell his car so as to be able to travel more!

To conjugate the conditional tense, you use the stem of the future (which is the infinitive) and the endings of the imperfect as shown in the table. Remember that –*re* verbs lose the final –*e* off the infinitive before you add the endings.

Conditional tense of *regarder* to watch		
Pronoun	**Ending**	**Example**
je (I)	–*ais*	*regarderais*
tu (you, sing.)	–*ais*	*regarderais*
il/elle (he/she)	–*ait*	*regarderait*
nous (we)	–*ions*	*regarderions*
vous (you, pl.)	–*iez*	*regarderiez*
ils (they, masc.) /*elles* (they, fem.)	–*aient*	*regarderaient*

Learning your tenses

There are various ways to go about learning your French verb tenses. The following methods are very useful:

▶ copying out your notes

▶ creating different-coloured mind maps of each tense

▶ memorising the rules from this book or your class notes

▶ completing lots of grammar exercises and practising them online.

You can practise your grammar online at these websites:

www.languagesonline.org.uk

www.uni.edu/becker/french31.html

www.realfrench.net/grammar

Mind maps

You could create different types of mind maps for each tense, putting the verb tense in the middle and the conjugations around it. Make sure that you write all of the words in capital letters, as this makes the words stand out. Since it takes you longer to write the words like this, you will think about it a bit more and are more likely to remember them. It also stops you from becoming lazy with your handwriting. It is important to use a variety of colours when creating your mind maps because then your work becomes much more attractive and, since most people enjoy colouring in, it also keeps you motivated. Here is an example of how you could do your mind map:

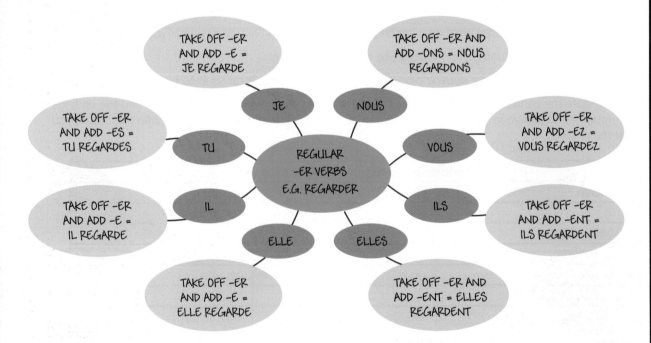

However, mind maps are a personal thing which work better when they stem from your own creativity, so try to think of your own layout if you can.

Notecards

One of the most effective ways to learn is by using notecards. If you follow these instructions carefully, you will know all of the main tenses off by heart very quickly.

1 Cut up lots of small pieces of card (preferably in different colours).

2 On one colour write down the pronouns *je, tu, il, elle, on, nous, vous, ils* and *elles*. Then add *mon ami, ma mère, Pierre et moi, Suzanne et Nicolas* and *les chats*.

3 On a second colour, write down ten regular *–er, –ir* and *–re* verbs. These cards can also be used to practise the present, the imperfect, the future and the conditional tenses.

4 On a third colour, write down all of the present tense irregular verbs that you find in this book.

5 On a fourth colour, write down ten verbs that take *avoir* in the past and ten that take *être*.

6 Now lay the pronouns face down on a table, floor or bed and lay one other set of cards next to them.

7 Take one card from each pile, for example you might choose *je* and *regarder*. Now conjugate the verb in the chosen tense. In the present tense, the example would be *je regarde*, in the future it would be, *je regarderai*. Check the notes in this book to see whether you conjugated the verb correctly.

8 Put the cards to the bottom of the pile, turn over the next two cards and repeat the process. Keep practising with the next two, and so on.

This exercise can be fun, especially when you do it with other people and you will find that you learn the tenses much more quickly than simply by reading your notes. You could even use a snakes and ladders game to make it more interesting when playing with friends: to go up a ladder, you need to conjugate a verb and if you go down a snake, you need to conjugate one as a forfeit.

Dice games

You can also make up dice games, such as the one below, to learn the tenses.

–er verbs

Roll No. 1	Roll No. 2
1 *je*	1 *regarder* (to watch)
2 *tu*	2 *monter* (to go up)
3 *il/elle*	3 *rentrer* (to return)
4 *nous*	4 *écouter* (to listen)
5 *vous*	5 *chercher* (to look for)
6 *ils/elles*	6 *réveiller* (to wake)

Roll the dice twice and then form a verb. For example, 3 + 4 = *Il écoute*.

Use the regular and irregular verbs of various tenses to invent games like this for yourself and your friends to play.

Singing

Another useful strategy is to sing the tenses in time to your favourite songs. This takes some concentration but it is possible and the advantage is, once you have tried it a couple of times, just playing that particular song will bring it all back to you without you even trying too hard to remember what you have learned. For example, imagine you are trying to learn the verb *être* (to be) and the song you like is 'Sound of the Underground' by Girls Aloud. The words of the chorus are:

It's the sound of the underground

The beat of the drum goes round and round

In to the overflow

Where the girls get down to the sound of the radio

Out to the electric night

Where the bass line jumps in the backstreet lights

The beat goes around and round

It's the sound of the under

Sound of the underground

continued

Singing – continued

But you are going to say the verb *être* instead, like this:

It's the sound of the underground
(je suis, tu es, il est)

The beat of the drum goes round and round
(elle est, nous sommes, vous êtes, ils sont)

In to the overflow
(elles sont, je suis, tu es)

Where the girls get down to the sound of the radio
(il est, elle est, nous sommes, vous êtes, ils sont, elles sont)

Out to the electric night
(je suis, tu es, il est)

Where the bass line jumps in the backstreet lights
(elle est, nous sommes, vous êtes, ils sont, elles sont)

The beat goes around and round
(je suis, tu es, il est, elle est)

It's the sound of the under
(nous sommes, vous êtes)

Sound of the underground.
(ils sont, elles sont)

You can learn three or four tenses using the same song for variation. For example, keep the chorus as the verb *être* but use *avoir* for verse one, *faire* for verse two and *aller* for verse three.

Introduction to dictionary use

You may find using a bilingual dictionary daunting at first because it is very different from the monolingual English dictionaries that you are used to. Not only is the dictionary in two parts (French–English and English–French), but each word may have a variety of translations and you need to choose the meaning which best fits the context of the text you are reading. Also, although it is unlikely to be the case, you may get the impression that lots of the words you need are missing from the dictionary. This is because when you come across a word in a passage which you need to look up, the dictionary entry for that word may be in a slightly different form. A verb, for example, will be in the infinitive and you may need to conjugate it after looking it up, in order to grasp the true meaning of the word or sentence. Due to these differences, many students misuse their dictionaries; they lose marks and do not achieve the grades they deserve. This chapter teaches you strategies for looking up words and phrases so that you can use your dictionary confidently. With good dictionary skills you will be able to answer the Reading questions accurately and clearly, as well as produce first class Folio pieces.

Four basic things to remember

1 This may seem obvious, but make sure you remember that the French words that you need to look up for the Reading are in the first half of the dictionary, while those that you need to look up in English to find the French are in the second half. Under the stressful conditions of a Reading exam, it is easy to spend precious minutes of your time searching frantically for a French word in the English section. So be careful!

2 Remember your alphabet! Although you will remember things like 's' comes before 't' and 'n' comes after 'm', when you look up a word like *stade* (stadium), it is easy to start at the 'sa–' section instead of flicking ahead towards the end of the 's' section.

3 When you have found the correct entry, skim over the information that comes before the definition that you need. For example, when looking up *couper* you will get (**kupe**) which tells you how to pronounce it; then ***conjug 1***, which tells you that it is a regular –*er* verb; then **1 vt**, which indicates that it is a transitive verb; then (**=sectionner**) which provides a synonym of the word in French. When writing your Folio pieces, it will be useful to know whether the word is a verb, or whether it is masculine or feminine but for the Reading, you can simply skip ahead to the English translation that you recognise.

4 Make sure that you choose the meaning that makes sense in the context of the rest of the sentence, not just the first translation that you find. For example, if you look up the verb *faire*, you will get the meanings 'make' and 'do' amongst others; if your sentence is *je dois faire mes devoirs*, then you have to translate *faire* as 'do', since the correct translation is unlikely to be 'I need to make my homework'. Therefore, check through all the possible meanings in your dictionary entry and consider carefully which one to choose.

Look out for

Think of each half of the dictionary as a separate dictionary in itself to give yourself a better estimate of where the word you are looking for will be.

Looking up nouns and adjectives

When looking up nouns and adjectives, you need to consider:

▶ gender (whether the word is masculine or feminine)

▶ number (whether the word is singular or plural).

This is always true for adjectives. Remember that adjectives change to agree with the noun they are describing, so you have to be very careful to look up the correct word in the dictionary, as it may not be printed exactly as you see it in the passage. When looking up nouns from English to French, for example when writing your essay, you will need to know which article to put before the word.

Nouns: French–English

Try these examples.

le traîneau

This one is easy. Go to the first half of your dictionary and find the 't' section. When you have found the 't's, flick to the end of the section and look for the 'tr' words. You should find *traîneau* near the start of the section. So, what does it mean? 'Sledge' or 'sleigh'!

les larmes

This time your noun is plural. You will not find *larmes* exactly like this in the dictionary, as the entry will be printed without the –s. So, look it up at the start of the 'l' section since the second letter is an 'a'. You will find that it means 'tear'. Remember, though, that the word was plural in French, so you will have to make it plural in English. Your translation will be 'tears' not 'tear'.

l'appuie-bras

Do not be put off by the fact that the word is hyphenated! You look these types of words up in the same way, but make sure that you go to the 'a' section of the dictionary, not the 'l'. You always miss out the article even when it is joined onto the noun like this. You will find *appuie-bras* towards the middle of the 'a' section because the second letter is 'p'. First of all you will come across *appuie* on its own (which means 'support'), then you will come across *appuie-bras*. What does it mean? 'Arm-rest'.

Nouns: English–French

Here are some examples of English words:

castle

Look up the English word 'castle' in the second half of the dictionary. You will find that the French translation for castle is *château* and that the word is followed by the letter '*m*'. This means that it is masculine and you will need to write *le* or *un* before it.

doctor

Do the same for this one, looking it up in the 'd' section of the dictionary. Again after the word, you will see the letter '*m*', which means it's masculine and once again you need to write *le* or *un* before the word.

leg

You probably know this word already, but if you were to look it up, you would use the second half of the dictionary again and look in the '*l*' section. You will find the word *jaube*. This time you can see the letter '*f*' after it, which means it's feminine, so you write *la* or *une* before the word.

Adjectives

laid

As for the French nouns, go to the first half of the dictionary and look the word up in the '*l*' section. You will find it translated as the English word 'ugly'.

paresseuse

This word is not quite so simple. Try looking for the word in the usual way. You will find that it is not there. That is because this adjective is in its feminine form and the ending has changed. Can you see a word that looks similar? The word *paresseux* which means 'lazy'.

blanches

The same thing happens when you look up this word. However, this time the adjective is both plural and irregular feminine so it has –he and an –s added. However, you can find the word *blanc* which, of course, means 'white'.

Looking up verbs

You may find looking up verbs one of the more challenging aspects of *Standard Grade French*. When you try to look up a verb that you find in the Reading, such as *cherche*, you will not see it in exactly this form. This is because dictionary entries for verbs are printed in the infinitive, or full form, of the verb. In this case, you would look up *chercher*. Remember that the infinitive of a verb always ends in *–er, –ir* or *–re* (see Chapter 1 Language skills). If you are struggling to find the verb you need in the dictionary, try looking for similar words which take one of these three endings.

For the following words, write down:

a)   the infinitive of the verb

b)   what the verb means

c)   what the actual translation is.

For example, *je regarde a) regarder,* b) to look, c) I look.

General Question 1

1 *(il) voit*

2 *(elle) habite*

3 *(tu) essayes*

4 *(je m)'inscris* (Because this verb has *m'*, it is reflexive and you must add *–s* to the infinitive that you find. However, you still look for the verb in the 'i' section.)

5 *(nous nous) habillons* (Another reflexive verb!)

6 *(ils) sont* (Your dictionary will tell you to *voir* (see) another word, to get the meaning of this. Look it up and then think carefully about how to translate *sont*.)

7 *(elles) font* (You have to change this word quite a bit to find it in the dictionary because it is irregular. However, as for question 6, your dictionary may tell you which word to look up to get the meaning. Make sure you know how to conjugate this verb before you sit your exam (see Chapter 1 Language skills)!

8 *(vous) reçevez*

For your Folio essays, you will need to look up verbs from English to French. This will be easier, as you simply need to conjugate the infinitive that you find. For example, you want to know how to say 'we go', so you look up 'go' and get *aller*; then you remember that the word for 'we' is *nous* and change the ending of the verb so that it agrees with the *nous* form (*–er* changed to *–ons*). Refer back to Chapter 1 Language skills for help with this.

Words that have more than one meaning

Although you may have got looking up French words and finding the English meanings down to a fine art by now, problems may arise when a word in French has more than one meaning in English, or when the same word appears as both a noun and a verb. For example, the word *livre* means both 'book' and 'pound' whilst *marche* means 'step' and any of 'I', 'he' or 'she walk(s)'. Therefore, you need to pay close attention to the context of the passage to work out which translation would be best in each case.

Read the sentences below and for each question, decide which is the best way to translate the words in bold.

General Question 2

1 *Hier, j'ai lu un bon **livre** qui s'appellait*
   Le Petit Prince.
   a) pound
   b) book

2 *En été je vais **passer** trois semaines en France.*
   a) spend
   b) sit/take
   c) pass

3 *Pour aller chez son copain à Aberdeen, il faut lire la **carte**.*
   a) menu
   b) map

4 ***Ferme** la fenêtre.*
   a) shut
   b) farm

5 *Mon **lit** est très grand et confortable.*
   a) bed
   b) reads

6 *La **langue** française est compliquée mais belle.*
   a) tongue
   b) language

7 *Je **cours** vite pour perdre du poids.*
   a) run
   b) class

8 *Il **porte** un costume qui fait rire.*
   a) carries
   b) wears

Although you probably got most of these questions correct, you may find it more difficult when it comes to looking up the words for yourself. Try these two on your own. Write down the two options for the meanings of the words in bold and then note which one is the most appropriate translation.

General Question 3

1 *Prends une **feuille** de papier du tiroir.*

a) Two meanings: _____   _____

b) Correct answer: _____

2 ***Fais** une tarte aux pommes avec les ingrédients suivants.*

a) Two meanings: _____   _____

b) Correct answer: _____

Looking up longer words and phrases

When confronted with longer words and phrases it is tempting to wade through the dictionary looking up every word along the way. However, you will not have the time to do this in an exam situation, nor is it necessary. The best way to tackle longer phrases is to pick out the key words which you think will allow you to figure out the general meaning.

Example 1

> *L'homme qui ne faisait pas du tout attention à la route parce qu'il était au téléphone, est rentré dans la barrière et l'a enfoncée.*

1 Before looking up any words in this sentence, see if you can work out what some of them mean without the dictionary. You should be able to guess *attention*, *téléphone* and *barrière* since they are similar in English. Are there any other words that you already know?

2 If not, which ones do you think would help you best understand this sentence? The key words to look up are: *route*, *rentré* and *enfoncée*.

3 Look these key words up in your dictionary, bearing in mind the guidelines given in this chapter.

route 'road' (noun)

rentré (verb in past tense, look up ending in −er), *rentrer* means 'to come back' but *rentrer dans* means 'to crash into'

enfoncée (verb in past tense, look up ending in −er), means 'to drive in; to smash; to sink into'; the extra −e shows that it is feminine and describes what happened to *la barrière*.

4 Now that you have worked out the key words, can you make sense of the sentence? Think about it, then check the answers.

Example 2

Je suis très inquiet à l'idée de rater tous mes examens en dépit de mes efforts pour étudier regulièrement.

Now repeat the process with this sentence. Which words can you guess? *Examens* 'exams', *effort* 'effort', *regulièrement* 'regularly'. Which are your key words? *Inquiet, rater, dépit.* Look them up. You will find these meanings:

inquiet 'worried'

rater 'to fail' (the verb is already in the infinitive form)

dépit 'despite' (you should find the whole phrase *en dépit de* which means 'in spite of' or 'despite'. On its own it means 'vexation' but this does not make sense here. Remember to check your dictionary thoroughly to make sure you get the right translation.

Example 3

Son père devrait soutenir son rêve de devenir chanteuse professionnelle mais, au contraire, il insiste pour qu'elle étudie le droit à l'université.

Look out for

Remember not to translate your sentences word for word, but in a way that makes sense and reads well in English. If you cannot understand your own sentence, then it will more than likely be marked wrong in the exam!

Try this example on your own using all of the steps above, then check the translation to see how accurate you were.

The Reading Paper

An analysis of recent General and Credit Reading papers shows that the most commonly asked question types are those where you:

▶ complete the sentences in English

▶ tick True or False

▶ tick the box

▶ write down someone's name

▶ mention one thing

▶ mention a number of things.

1 We will explore each of these question types in more detail later in this chapter.

2 In the General paper, **all six** types of question can be asked, whereas the Credit paper usually asks only **two** types: 'mention one thing', or 'mention a number of things'.

The other main difference between the two papers is the amount of information that you need to give. You will find that the General paper has more questions, but that they are broken down into manageable chunks. The Credit paper has fewer questions but they need longer answers.

In the exam, you should read each question carefully. Use the marks available for each answer as a guide to how much information to give. For longer Reading passages, the order the questions are asked in gives a clue as to where in the text your answer is likely to be. Key words can then help you to pinpoint the precise details you need for your answer.

This chapter will take you through each type of question, based on examples from Past Papers. Worked examples show you how to tackle each type of question, and then you can try an example for yourself. Before testing yourself against the examples, make sure you learn the list of 'false friends' and the list of 'signalling' words which follow.

'False friends'

'False friends' are words which look like an English word but have a different meaning. Here is a list of the most common false friends. Read them carefully and learn them off by heart. It is important to know these words so that you do not misinterpret the Reading passages or waste precious time in the exam by looking them up in the dictionary.

False friends

actuellement	at the moment	*lecture*	reading
ancien(ne)	old, former	*librairie*	bookshop
assister à	to attend, to be present at	*location*	rental
blesser	to injure	*monnaie*	change, coins
car	coach	*nuisance*	harm, damage
cave	cellar	*pièce*	room, a play
chance	luck	*prévenir*	to warn
chef	boss	*professeur*	teacher
collège	school	*prune*	plum
coin	corner	*raisin*	grape
commander	to order	*réaliser*	to achieve, to carry out
conducteur	driver	*réunion*	meeting
contrôler	to check	*sensible*	sensitive
déception	disappointment	*supporter*	to put up with
demander	to ask for	*sympa(thique)*	nice
avoir envie de	to want, to feel like	*travailler*	to work
gentil(le)	kind	*veste*	jacket
habit	dress, clothes		
ignorer	not to know		
journée	day		

Look out for

Once you know the false friends, it is relatively safe to assume that any other words which look like English words do have the same meaning. Only look these up if you have extra time at the end of the exam.

'Signalling' words

Certain conjunctions (for example, 'but', 'because', 'since') can completely change the meaning of a sentence. Look at the following sentences.

*J'ai acheté un pull **et** j'ai acheté un jean.*

*J'ai acheté un pull **mais** je **n'ai pas** acheté un jean.*

What is the difference in meaning? The first sentence says 'I bought jeans' and the second says 'I didn't buy jeans.' The words *et* (and) and *mais* (but) are very important as they give you a clue straight away to the direction the sentence is taking. The conjunction *et* signals that extra information will be given, while the use of *mais* alerts you to an obstacle or difficulty of some kind. Perhaps a contrary opinion or a problem will be mentioned next. Remember that *ne ... pas* around a verb means 'not', 'doesn't', 'didn't' or 'no' and makes a sentence negative.

Here is a list of important 'signalling' words to look out for. You may find these especially useful for the longer Credit Reading passages. Try to learn them off by heart.

Signalling words

afin que	so that	*mais/or*	but
aussi	also	*ne ... pas*	not, no, doesn't, didn't
aussitôt que	as soon as		
bien que	although	*néanmoins*	nevertheless
cependant/pourtant	however	*ou*	or
comme	like/as	*où*	where
donc/alors	so	*parce que/car*	because
d'où	hence	*pourvu que*	provided that
en dépit de	despite	*puisque/vu que*	since
et	and	*si*	if

Checklist of skills for the Reading paper

If you can answer 'Yes' to each of the following skills in the checklist, then you are ready to tackle the Reading paper.

	Checklist	Done
1	I know what *avoir* and *être* mean and can form these verbs in the present tense. (See Chapter 1)	
2	I understand how to form *–er*, *–ir* and *–re* verbs in the present, perfect, future and conditional tenses. (See Chapter 1)	
3	I can recognise all of the irregular verbs in the present, perfect, future and conditional tenses. (See Chapter 1)	
4	I know how to look up different words and phrases in a French dictionary. (See Chapter 2)	
5	I'm aware of the main 'false friends' in French and know most of them off by heart. (See page 44)	
6	I understand what the main 'signalling' words mean. (See page 44)	

Complete the sentences in English

Questions where you complete the sentences in English are very common. Recently, about one third of the questions in the General papers have been of this type.

The best method for handling this type of question is:

1 Read the incomplete English sentences under the French passage and highlight (or circle) the key English words.

2 Then go to the French passage and underline the French translations for your key words. (If you do not know the French for these words, look them up in the second half of your dictionary.)

3 Check the text in the French passage directly after (or near to) these words and see if you can work out the meaning. Use your dictionary if you need to.

4 Once you are clear about the meaning, complete the sentences in English.

For this type of question, notice that there is one key word per sentence. The function of the key word is to help you identify the part of the passage with the answer.

Now look at the Past Paper question on the page opposite, and put the method above into practice!

General Example 1
(2004 General Reading Q3)

4. Then you read the advice given to the girl.

Conseil

Chère Adrienne!

Il y a beaucoup de filles qui sont comme toi. A ton âge, c'est normal. Tu peux commencer en lui parlant des choses que vous avez en commun, comme les devoirs, les jeux-vidéo que tu préfères etc.

Complete the sentences. 2

She is told that many girls _are like her_ .

She should talk to him about _things they have in common_ .

_____ .

Read the paragraph and look at the sentences you have to complete.

1 Your key words are: girls, talk.

2 The matching French words in the passage are: girls *filles*, talk *parlant*. (If you do not know these words, use your dictionary.)

3 The text straight after these words reads: *filles qui sont comme toi. À ton âge, c'est normal...* and *parlant des choses que vous avez en commun...* Try to work out what these phrases mean. Again, use your dictionary if you need to.

4 For the first phrase, the words *comme* and *toi* are in the dictionary. For *sont*, your dictionary will say *voir être*. The verb *être* (to be) is irregular and you would be best off knowing this verb. You can work out that Adrienne is told 'many girls are like you.'

For the second phrase, you could probably guess that *en commun* means 'in common' and *choses* (things) is easy to find in the dictionary. *Vous avez* means 'you (plural) have'. Rather than being redirected to the irregular verb *avoir*, it is easier to learn it. Adrienne is advised to talk to him about 'things you have in common'.

Look out for

Make sure that you know the irregular verbs *avoir* (to have) and *être* (to be) off by heart. As well as being used on their own, these verbs form the tenses.

Look out for

Remember that you may need to look up the stem of the word in the dictionary, rather than the exact form used in the passage, because verbs, adjectives and nouns change according to their subject. If you cannot find a word, look for a similar one. For example, you will find the verb *parler* (to speak) rather than the present form *parlant* (speaking). You will find the singular noun chose (thing) rather than the plural *choses* (things).

General Example 2
(2005 General Reading Q6)

---

6. There is an article about a chef.

> ### *Chef cuisinier et patron de restaurant!*
> ### *Louis Picaud raconte sa journée!*
>
> Alors, chaque matin je vais choisir mes poissons et ma viande au marché. Quand je reviens, je prépare la carte du jour et on commence à travailler dans la cuisine. Il y a deux services, à midi et à dix-neuf heures. Le soir, je fais les comptes avec ma femme.
>
> J'ai commencé à quatorze ans. J'aidais mon père dans son restaurant. Puis, comme apprenti, j'ai travaillé dans les grands restaurants de plusieurs villes. J'ai appris á préparer les spécialités de toutes les régions.
>
> Ensuite j'ai ouvert mon propre restaurant et maintenant j'ai trois jeunes apprentis qui travaillent chez moi.

Complete the sentences.   5

In the mornings, Louis goes to the market to buy _____.

Then he prepares the day's _____.

In the evening his wife helps him with _____.

As an apprentice chef he worked in restaurants in _____.

Now he has _____.

Read the paragraph and look at the sentences you have to complete. Notice that there are five marks – one mark per question. This passage is slightly longer so you will need more time to find where the answers are in the text. The order in which the questions are asked indicates where in the passage the answers will be.

1 Your key words are: market, prepares, evening, restaurants, now.

2 Find the matching French words in the passage. You will either know or be able to guess most of them, but use your dictionary if necessary.

3 Then try to translate the phrases after these words.

4 Complete the sentences in English.

General Example 3
(2006 General Reading Q4)

Marks

4. You read an article about a disaster on the Pacific island of Fiji.

Pluies Torrentielles au Fidji

Hier, près de 8 000 personnes ont été obligées de quitter leurs maisons et de partir dans la haute terre de l'île principale du Fidji. C'est la suite de dix jours de pluie ininterrompue.

Huit personnes sont mortes, onze autres ont disparu.

Le gouvernement du pays a promis de l'aide financière pour les habitants qui ont perdu leurs domiciles.

Complete the sentences.   **4**

About 8000 (people) had to _____ .

The disaster was caused by (ten days) of _____ .

(Eleven) people have _____ .

The government will help (people) who _____ .

_____ .

Read this short paragraph carefully and then read the incomplete sentences in English. It is good practice to notice the marks available and the order the questions are asked in.

1 Your key words are: people, ten days, eleven, people.

2 Find the matching French words in the passage. In the last English sentence, the key word 'people' means 'inhabitant'. Be aware of the slight differences in meaning that the same word can have.

3 Then try to translate the phrases after these words.

4 Complete the sentences in English.

General Example 4
(2006 General Reading Q7)

Try this one on your own. Read the paragraph carefully and try to complete the sentences using the method you have been practising.

Marks

7. You read an article about travel.

> ## Tu aimes voyager?
>
> Selon un sondage, huit enfants sur dix sont déjà partis à l'étranger et environ 40% d'entre eux partent chaque année. Les destinations les plus populaires sont l'Europe, suivi des Etats-Unis et de l'Afrique.
>
> En général les enfants ont envie de découvrir d'autres pays et de faire la connaissance d'autres personnes.

Complete the sentences.

(a) 8 children in 10 have _____   1

_____ .

(b) Europe, USA and Africa are _____   1

_____ .

(c) In general children like discovering other countries and _____   1

_____ .

General Example 5
(2007 General Reading Q2)

Now try this one!

Marks

2. A boy has written to the magazine about a girl he met.

> ## Je n'ai pas fait le premier pas!
>
> J'ai un petit problème. J'ai fait la connaissance d'une fille superbe, quand j'étais en vacances au bord de la mer. On s'est bien amusé, mais je n'ai pas eu le courage de lui dire que je l'aime. Rentré chez moi, je pense tout le temps à elle. Que faire?
>
> *Martin, 14 ans*

Complete the sentences.   3

Martin met the girl when he was _____ .

He didn't have the courage to tell her that _____ .

Now that he's back home he _____ .

Tick True or False

True or False questions come up frequently in the General Reading paper but not in the Credit paper. You can use the same method for these questions as for 'Complete the sentences in English' (see page 46). However, notice that for these questions there are several key words per sentence rather than one. The purpose of these key words is to test the truth of the statements, rather than to find the right part of the text.

When you are unsure of some of the translation, the presence of all (or most) of the key words will help to confirm whether or not the statements are correct. Remember to read the statements carefully and to tick the box that is most likely to be the answer, even if you are not certain. This may seem really obvious, but lots of candidates leave this section blank.

Have a look at the first Tick True or False question over the page, and see how you get on with this question type.

General Example 1
(2004 General Reading Q8)

Read the following passage and look at the True or False sentences.

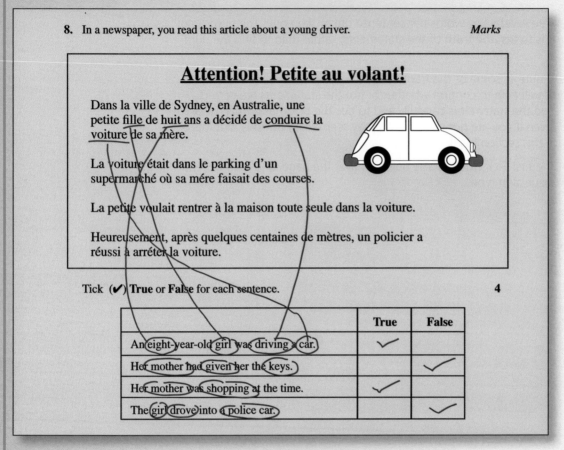

8. In a newspaper, you read this article about a young driver.   *Marks*

Attention! Petite au volant!

Dans la ville de Sydney, en Australie, une petite fille de huit ans a décidé de conduire la voiture de sa mère.

La voiture était dans le parking d'un supermarché où sa mére faisait des courses.

La petite voulait rentrer à la maison toute seule dans la voiture.

Heureusement, après quelques centaines de mètres, un policier a réussi à arrêter la voiture.

Tick (✔) **True** or **False** for each sentence.   **4**

	True	False
An eight-year-old girl was driving a car.	✔	
Her mother had given her the keys.		✔
Her mother was shopping at the time.	✔	
The girl drove into a police car.		✔

1 The first English sentence states that an eight-year-old girl was driving the car. Your key words are: eight, girl, driving and car.

2 See if you can find the matching French words in the text. They are: eight *huit*, girl *fille*, to drive *conduire* and car *voiture*.

3 Try to translate the sentence with these words. If you are not quite sure of the sense, the fact that all of these words are in the text indicates that the sentence is true. The only time that it would be false is if the negative *ne ... pas* was surrounding the verb *conduire*.

4 Tick the box for True.

Use the same method for the next English sentence. Your key words are: mother, given, keys. The French words for these are: mother *mère*, to give *donner*, keys *clés*. The only one of these words in the text is *mère*, so you can assume that the statement is false.

The key words for the third English sentence are: mother, shopping. The French words for these are: mother *mère*, shopping *courses* (or *achats*). Do either of these words appear in the text? Yes, both of them do. Therefore the sentence is true.

In the fourth sentence, the key words are: girl, drive, police car. The French translations are: *fille, conduire, voiture de police*. This sentence is a bit trickier because the words in the text are similar to the key words, but they are not exactly the same. The text says that a policeman stopped the car that the girl was driving. Therefore the sentence is false.

General Example 2
(2005 General Reading Q10)

Using the same approach, try doing this question yourself.

10. You read about the French sprinter, Muriel Hurtis.

Muriel Hurtis – athlète extraordinaire!

Muriel Hurtis est née le 25 mars, 1979. Elle grandit en Seine-Saint-Denis dans la région parisienne. Au collège, elle découvre l'athlétisme par hasard. Un jour, elle va au stade avec une copine et le prof de sport la voit.

En 1998, Muriel obtient son baccalauréat en sciences. Cette année-là, elle gagne une médaille d'or sur 200 mètres aux Championnats du Monde Juniors à Annecy – son premier succès public.

Tick (✔) **True** or **False** for each sentence.   3

	True	False
Muriel got into athletics by chance.		
Her PE teacher took her to the stadium one day.		
In 1998, she won a gold medal for the 200 metres.		

Tick the box

You can apply the same approach to Tick the box questions as to the True or False questions: find the key words and tick the box which contains the key words from the passage. As with the True or False questions, there are a number of key words per sentence. When the French words for these are present in the passage, this serves to test the truth of the statements.

General Example 1
(2005 General Reading Q9)

Read the following passage and look at the statements.

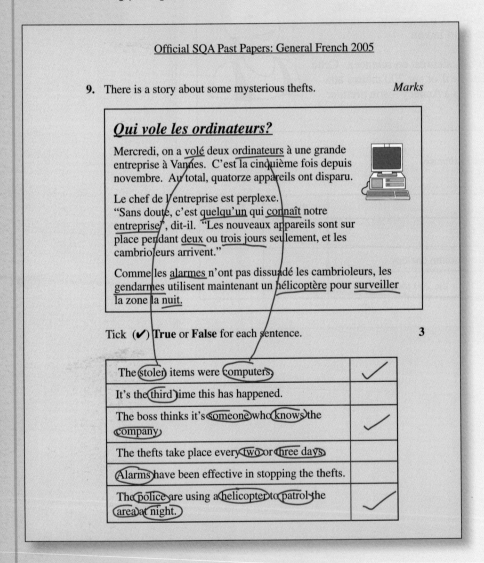

Official SQA Past Papers: General French 2005

9. There is a story about some mysterious thefts.   *Marks*

Qui vole les ordinateurs?

Mercredi, on a volé deux ordinateurs à une grande entreprise à Vannes. C'est la cinquième fois depuis novembre. Au total, quatorze appareils ont disparu.

Le chef de l'entreprise est perplexe. "Sans doute, c'est quelqu'un qui connaît notre entreprise", dit-il. "Les nouveaux appareils sont sur place pendant deux ou trois jours seulement, et les cambrioleurs arrivent."

Comme les alarmes n'ont pas dissuadé les cambrioleurs, les gendarmes utilisent maintenant un hélicoptère pour surveiller la zone la nuit.

Tick (✔) **True** or **False** for each sentence.   3

The stolen items were computers.	✓
It's the third time this has happened.	
The boss thinks it's someone who knows the company.	✓
The thefts take place every two or three days.	
Alarms have been effective in stopping the thefts.	
The police are using a helicopter to patrol the area at night.	✓

1 Were the stolen items computers, as stated in the first English sentence? Your key words are: steal, computers.

2 The French for these key words would be: to steal *voler*, computers *ordinateurs*. The infinitive form of the verb *voler* (to steal) is not in the passage but the past tense *volé* (stolen) is there.

3 The title of the passage reads *Qui vole les ordinateurs?* (Who is stealing the computers?) and the first sentence states *on a volé deux ordinateurs ...* (someone has stolen two computers ...). If you are unsure of the translation, the presence of both the key words in the passage indicates that the statement is correct.

4 The statement is correct, so tick the first box.

How many times this has happened? Key word: third *troisième*. Neither *troisième* nor *trois* (three) are in the text. The text says *C'est la cinquième fois ...* (It is the fifth time ...) Therefore this statement is incorrect and you should leave the box blank.

Does the boss think that the thief is someone who knows the company? Key words: someone, know, company. The French for these words is: *quelqu'un, connaît, entreprise*. Are these words in the passage? Yes, so tick this box.

Do the thefts take place every two or three days? Key words: theft *vol*, two *deux*, three *trois*, day *jour*. Are all these words in the text? Yes, but when you read the text carefully, the word *vol* (theft) is not mentioned in connnection with the other key words. Instead, the text says *Les nouveaux appareils sont sur place pendant deux ou trois jours ...* (The new computers are in place for two or three days ...) Therefore the statement is incorrect and you should leave this box blank.

Have the alarms have been effective in stopping the thefts? Key words: alarms *alarmes*, stop *arrêter*, theft *vol*. At this point in the text, *alarmes* is the only key word used but other vocabulary is used to describe the events and you may need your dictionary: *dissuader* (to put off), *cambrioleurs* (burglars) – similar key words are there. However, notice that the negative form is used: **n'ont pas** *dissuadé*. The sentence means that 'the alarms did not put the burglars off'. So leave this box blank as well.

For the sixth and last statement you need to find out whether the police have been using a helicopter to patrol the area by night. (You can work out that you must tick this box as you have only ticked two so far and the instructions say you must tick three.) Your key words are: police *gendarmes*, helicopter *hélicoptère*, patrol *surveiller*, area *zone*, night *nuit*. The only word here that you may not be able to guess is the word for 'police'. All of these words are in the passage so tick this box.

Look out for

Remember, you always have to look up verbs in their **infinitive** form in the dictionary.

General Example 2
(2006 General Reading Q2)

Now try doing this question yourself following the same method.

Marks

2. There is an article in the magazine about bringing a beach to Paris.

Une Plage à Paris

Pendant les quatre semaines du mois d'août, les Parisiens ont une plage chez eux.

Le maire de Paris a fait apporter des tonnes de sable sur les bords de la rivière Seine. On a apporté aussi des chaises, des parasols et des palmiers.

On ne peut pas nager, car l'eau est trop polluée, mais il y a des jets d'eau pour rafraîchir le public. Le soir, on propose des spectacles, et même des dîners!

Tick (✓) the **three** correct sentences.

3

There will be a beach in Paris for two weeks in August.	
Tons of sand have been brought to the river Seine.	
There are also seats, parasols and palm trees.	
People will be able to swim in the river.	
Jets of water will be used to clean the sand.	
At night there will be shows and dinners.	

Write down someone's name

This type of question is typical of a General Reading paper. The method for handling it is the same as that outlined for the other General questions. Read the statements carefully and work out which key words to look for. The purpose of the key words in these questions is to help you find the right passage.

General Example 1
(2004 General Reading Q1)

You are reading a French magazine.

Marks

1. Some primary school pupils give their opinions about school.

<u>Que penses-tu de l'école?</u>

Moi, j'aime aller à l'école pour les copains. La maîtresse est gentille, mais ce que je préfère vraiment, c'est la récréation!

Guillaume, 8 ans

J'aime ma maîtresse. Elle explique très bien et j'apprends beaucoup de choses avec elle. J'aime bien l'école, mais mon Papa et ma Maman me manquent.

Jacqueline, 9 ans

A l'école, je préfère le calcul et et l'histoire. Mais, parfois, c'est fatigant aussi. J'aimerais avoir des consoles et des jeux-vidéo.

Paulette, 10 ans

Je n'aime pas l'école parce que je n'aime pas travailler. C'est ennuyeux. Je préfère rester chez moi jouer avec mon chien.

Jean-Luc, 8 ans

Which of the pupils said the following?

3

Sometimes school is tiring.

What I really like is the morning break.

I'd rather stay at home.

Paulette

Guillaume

Jean-Luc

1 For the first statement, the key words are: sometimes, school, tiring.

2 The French for these words is: sometimes *parfois*, school *école*, tiring *fatigant*. Can you find a passage which contains these words? (If you cannot recognise any of them, you will need to use your dictionary.)

3 Each of the passages uses the word *école* but only Paulette says *Mais, parfois, c'est fatigant aussi.*

4 Write down Paulette for the first statement.

The key words in the second statement are: I like (*j'aime* or *je préfère*) and break *récréation*. Three of the passages use either the phrase *j'aime* or *je préfère* but only Guillaume mentions *la récréation*. Guillaume is the answer.

The key words in the third statement are: I'd rather *je préfère* , to stay *rester* and home *maison/chez moi*. The answer is Jean-Luc.

General Example 2
(2007 General Reading Q3)

Marks

3. You read about a group of Spanish pupils who visited a school in France. Here are the opinions of some of the French pupils about the visit.

Des Espagnols en Bourgogne

Au début, nous, on parlait français et eux, ils parlaient espagnol. C'était assez difficile, mais on s'exprimait par gestes.

Noël

On a fait des progrès. Maintenant je sais quelques mots en espagnol. Je me suis fait beaucoup de copines et on s'écrit souvent maintenant.

Emeline

On était soixante jeunes. Le soir on faisait des jeux et on avait du temps libre quand on était seuls sans les adultes.

Gerald

Who said the following? Write the correct name beside each statement.   **4**

There were 60 young people.	
I can say a few words in Spanish.	
We used gestures.	
We write to each other often.	

Mention one thing

Questions asking you for a specific piece of information come up frequently in both General and Credit Reading papers. To answer these questions, you need to be clear and concise. Giving one correct piece of information along with lots of incorrect information could still lose you the mark for that question!

General Example 1
(2004 General Reading Q2)

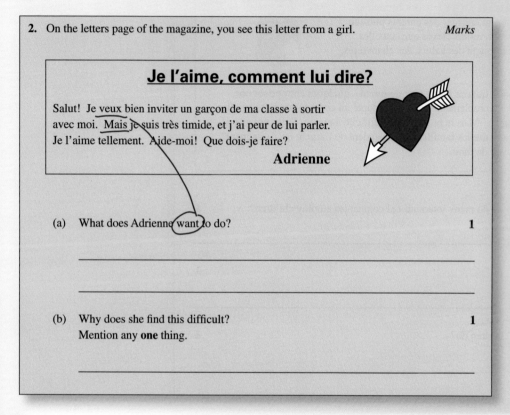

2. On the letters page of the magazine, you see this letter from a girl.   *Marks*

Je l'aime, comment lui dire?

Salut! Je veux bien inviter un garçon de ma classe à sortir avec moi. Mais je suis très timide, et j'ai peur de lui parler. Je l'aime tellement. Aide-moi! Que dois-je faire?

Adrienne

(a)   What does Adrienne want to do?   1

_____

_____

(b)   Why does she find this difficult?   1
       Mention any **one** thing.

_____

1 Question (a) asks 'What does Adrienne want to do?'. Your key word is the verb 'want'.

2 The French for 'I want' is *je veux*.

3 Try to work out what the rest of the sentence means. You can guess that *inviter* means 'to invite'; if you do not know that *garçon* means 'boy' you will find it in the dictionary; you can guess that *classe* means 'class'; *sortir* means 'to go out'; you should know that *moi* means 'me'. So the answer is that Adrienne wants to ask a boy in her class to go out with her.

4 This is the basic information that you need. Do not try to add anything else from any other section of the passage or make any guesses because you have already answered the question fully.

Question (b) asks 'Why does she find this difficult?'. The word 'difficult' alerts you to the fact that there's a problem with asking the boy out. The word *mais* (but) in the next French sentence does not translate the word 'difficult' but it signals that the reason for the problem will be given. You now need to find out what it is. You can guess that *timide* means 'shy'; look up *peur* (fear) if you need to; you should know the verb *parler* (to speak). Put all that together and you get 'She is shy and is scared to speak to him'. You only need to say one of these two points to get the mark, so mention the part that you are most sure about.

Credit Example 2
(2004 Credit Reading Q6)

This example is from a Credit Reading paper.

---

6. The article about working children goes on.   *Marks*

> Qui plus est, environ 10 millions sont employés dans les pays en voie de dévelopment par les grandes entreprises internationales qui préfèrent engager des enfants puisque leurs salaires sont, bien sûr, moins élevés que ceux des adultes. Ces enfants fabriquent des habits, des chaussures, des tapis.
>
> Grâce à des images chocs, qui ont fait le tour du monde, quelques entreprises ont voulu se présenter plus favorablement. Elles ont adopté un code de conduite, et elles n'emploient plus d'enfants. Mais le problème est difficile à régler. Si les enfants ne travaillent plus, que vont faire les familles qui dépendent de l'argent qu'ils gagnent? Ils risquent tous de mourir de faim.

(a)   In which countries do many international companies employ children?   1

_____

(b)   Why is this?   1

_____

(c)   What do these children do?   1

_____

(d)   What have these international companies now agreed to do?   1

_____

(e)   Why might this not bring a solution to the problem?   1

_____

1 For question (a) you need to find a type of country. Your key word is: country.

2 The French for 'country' is *pays*. Finding this word in the passage will take you to the right area of the text. After your key word, you see *en voie de développement*.

3 If you cannot guess what this means, use your dictionary. However, do not look up *en*, as you will probably find *en voie* under *voie* so try looking that up first. You can probably guess that *développement* means 'development'. If you translate the sentence word for word, you will find it means 'countries in the process of development'.

4 In English, this would be 'developing countries'.

To answer (b), you have to give a reason why they employ children, so the key word is 'children' *enfants*. The word *puisque* (since) comes directly after this word in the passage. It is used in the sense of 'because', so you can expect to find the reason following. You can guess that *salaire* means 'salary'; *moins* (less); *élevé* (high); *que* (than); *adultes* (adults). Translated into good English then, your answer is 'because children have lower salaries than adults'.

To answer (c), you have to find out what the children do, so your key word is 'children' *enfants* again. This time your answer can be found in the sentence: *Ces enfants fabriquent des chaussures, des habits, des tapis*. You may need to look up all the main words: *fabriquer* – not *fabriquent* because it is a verb! (to make); *chaussure* – without the 's' on the end because it is plural (shoes); *habit* (clothes) and *tapis* (carpets). The answer is that the children make shoes, clothes and carpets.

Try to answer (d) and (e) yourself, going through the same process.

Mention a number of things

These questions make up about 50 per cent of the Credit Reading paper. The best technique is to read the questions carefully, then go back to the text and underline where you think the answers can be found, and try to work out the meaning.

For each question, check the marks available. Use the number of marks as a guide to how much to write. For example, if the question is worth two marks, then you need to give two pieces of information; if it is worth three marks, then you should mention three things. Do **not** give more or less information than required or you may lose marks.

Credit Example 1
(2003 Credit Reading Q3)

---

3. You read an article about what houses will be like in the future.　　*Marks*

> **LA MAISON DU FUTUR**
>
> La technologie avance si vite. Qu'est-ce qu'on trouvera dans la maison de l'an 2020? Dans cette maison, un micro est relié à l'ordinateur qui contrôle toutes les fonctions de la maison.
>
> **La cuisine:**
> C'est un vrai paradis! Quand on a faim, on dit ce qu'on veut manger, et l'ordinateur donne non seulement la liste des ingrédients, mais aussi la méthode et le temps de cuisson. Et en plus, il allume la cuisinière et contrôle la température du four. Le soir, en rentrant du travail, on envoie un message électronique directement de sa voiture à l'ordinateur. Et voilà! Un plat chaud sera prêt quand on arrivera!
>
> **Le frigo:**
> Dès qu'on prend du lait, du fromage ou d'autres produits dans le frigo, l'ordinateur enregistre les codes-barres. Il note constamment le contenu du frigo, envoie des commandes au supermarché et puis le commerçant livre ce qui manque.

(a) A microphone will be connected to the "house" computer. What will happen when you tell the computer what you want to eat? Mention any **three** things.　　**3**

　　The computer will give the list of ingredients.
　　It will also give the method.
　　It will give the cooking time.

1　Read the question carefully. Then work out which key words you need to look for. Your key words are: computer, eat.

2　Look for *ordinateur* (computer) and *manger* (to eat). Underline these words in the passage.

3　Look at the section of the passage directly after these words and underline the sentence where you think the three things that will happen are listed: *et l'ordinateur donne non seulement la liste des ingrédients, mais aussi la méthode et le temps de cuisson. Et en plus, il allume la cuisinière et contrôle la température du four.* Read the text over again and see if you can guess roughly what it means. Look for words that look like English words (*liste, ingrédients, méthode, contrôle* and *température*) and think of the vocabulary you already know (*l'ordinateur, temps,* etc.). Now look up any words you are not sure of and write them down (for example, *donner* to give; *allumer* to switch on; *four* oven). If your answer does not make sense in English then it is wrong. Think of another way to word your answer so that it makes sense, and then write it down.

4　There are three marks, one mark for each of the three things you need to mention.

Credit Example 2
(2006 Credit Reading Q5)

Marks

5. You read an article in which young French people discuss whether machines are good or bad for society.

Les machines nous apportent des biens. Oui! Mais ......

Chantal: Prenons le téléphone, par exemple. Cela nous permet de parler à une personne qui se trouve à des dizaines, même des centaines, de kilomètres. C'est quelque chose qui facilite la vie, mais par conséquence, il y a moins de courrier et donc, moins de travail, et peut-être le chômage pour les facteurs.

Mathieu: Plus on a de machines, plus on a de besoins. Par exemple, on a inventé le portable. Mais, pour les faire fonctionner, on a besoin de chargeurs et d'un réseau.

Thierry: Et maintenant il y a les ordinateurs. Dans l'avenir, les ordinateurs feront tout le travail des hommes, mais les gens ne vont pas s'ennuyer. Au lieu de travailler, ils pourront consacrer tout leur temps à s'amuser.

(a) According to Chantal the telephone has been a useful invention. But, what are the disadvantages? Mention any **two** things.   2

There will be less mail.

Perhaps the postal workers will be out of work.

---

1 The question asks what the disadvantages of the telephone are. There are two marks available. Look for key words to introduce the disadvantages. The actual word 'disadvantage' does not appear but Chantal begins by describing the advantages and then says *mais* (but). As with the example on page 59 (2004 General Reading question 2), *mais* signals that problems and disadvantages may be mentioned next.

2 Underline the word *mais* (but).

3 Read the passage directly after this word and underline what you think the two disadvantages may be: *par conséquence, il y a moins de courrier et donc, moins de travail, et peut-être le chômage pour les facteurs.* See which words you recognise from the English (*courrier* mail) and which words you already know (*moins* less; *travail* work). Look up any words you do not know and write them down (for example, *chômage* unemployment; *facteurs* postmen). Think about what the text means and then write down an answer which makes sense in English. If you really have no idea, then guess!

4 There are two marks, one mark for each of the two things you need to mention.

Credit Example 3
(2007 Credit Reading Q4)

Marks

4. You then read an article about people who move to other countries.

POURQUOI QUITTER SON PAYS?

Un habitant du monde sur trente-cinq est immigré: une personne qui <u>quitte</u> <u>son pays</u> pour aller <u>vivre dans un pays plus développé, pour trouver du</u> <u>travail et de meilleures conditions de vie.</u> Mais beaucoup des pays qui les accueillent ne sont pas nécessairement riches. Souvent les entreprises et les usines sont en train de se développer et elles ont besoin d'employés.

Dans les pays d'accueil, ces immigrations peuvent poser des difficultés. Les immigrés s'installent parfois dans les régions où il y a moins de possibilités de travail et où il y a déjà beaucoup de chômage.

(a) Why does one person in 35 in the world (leave) his/her own (country)? Mention any **two** things.

2

_____

_____

Credit Example 4
(2005 Credit Reading Q4)

Read the following paragraph carefully and try to answer the question.

Robbie Williams ... une drôle de vie!

Marks

Robert Peter Williams est né le 13 février 1974 à Newcastle. Ses parents ont divorcé quand Robbie avait trois ans et après, il a vécu avec sa mère, Theresa. Il a aussi une soeur ainée, Sally.

C'est un neveu de sa soeur qui a trouvé pour Robbie son premier emploi: vendeur de fenêtres à double vitrage.

Les premières années de sa vie, il habitait une maison tout près d'un stade où s'entraînait Port Vale FC, son équipe préférée. A l'école, il etait plutôt bon élève, il avait toujours de bonnes notes dans la plupart des matières.

Comme son père, Robbie se destinait à la comédie, mais à l'âge de 16 ans, il a été engagé pour former le groupe Take That. Après avoir quitté le groupe très fâché contre le producteur, il s'est lancé dans une carrière solo qui a mis plusieurs années à démarrer. Voilà pourquoi il a sombré dans l'alcool et la drogue.

Libéré de ses démons, Robbie a signé avec sa maison de disques un énorme contrat qui l'abritera du besoin d'argent jusqu' à la fin de ses jours.

(a) What was Robbie's first job and how did he get it?

2

_____

_____

---

1 The key words are: leave, country.

2 The French for these words is: leave *quitter*, country *pays*. Underline the section where these words appear: *quitte son pays*.

3 Directly after the key words, underline what you think the two reasons may be: *pour aller vivre dans un pays plus développé, pour trouver du travail et de meilleures conditions de vie.* Which words are similar to the English? (*développé* developped; *conditions* conditions). Which words do you know? (*vivre* to live, *travail* work, *vie* life). Look up any words you do not know. Try and work out the meaning and write an answer that makes sense. If you are stuck, then guess.

4 There are two marks, one mark for each of the two things.

Credit Example 5
(2004 Credit Reading Q3)

Un aéroport de plus pour Paris?

Paris aura un troisième aéroport, après ceux d'Orly et de Roissy. Des sept sites possibles, c'est celui de Chaulnes, en Picardie, qui a été sélectionné. Selon les experts, cet endroit a le maximum d'advantages.

Situé à 125 kilomètres de Paris, il est relié à la capitale parl'autoroute et un Train à Grande Vitesse. Comme c'est une région peu peuplée, le survol des avions ne gênera pas trop de monde. C'est un avantage.

Mais le projet provoque beaucoup de crainte chez les habitants de la région. Ils estiment que le gouvernement a imposé son choix sans véritable discussion, et ils ne veulent pas subir le bruit et la pollution que le projet leur apportera.

(a) What transport links with Paris dooes the new site at Chaulnes, in Picardy, have?   **2**

Summary

▶ Always read the introduction to the questions.

▶ Now read the questions.

▶ Check the marks available.

▶ Know the number of points you are looking for.

▶ Skim read the passage for general understanding.

▶ Spot words and phrases that you know.

▶ Use the key word technique to pinpoint your answers.

▶ Only use a dictionary where necessary.

▶ Make sure your answers make sense.

▶ Fill in any blanks with educated guesses!

The Listening Paper

For the Listening paper you must listen to the sound of the French words to work out what they mean. You will not have the French text to refer to and you may **not** use a dictionary. You will need to 'think on your feet' as there is less time to reflect upon your answers. For these reasons, most students find this paper challenging. However, an advantage of the Listening extracts is that they are much shorter. Nearly everything you hear on the CD in the exam will be relevant to your answer and each recording will be played three times.

Like the Reading paper, the General Listening paper is made up of a variety of question types where you have to answer each one in a different way, using a different skill. The Credit Listening paper, on the other hand, is usually made up completely of questions where you have to write your own answers, mentioning either one thing or a number of things. An analysis of recent General and Credit Listening papers reveals that, like in the Reading paper, the most commonly asked question types are those where you:

▶ complete the sentences in English

▶ tick True or False

▶ tick the box

▶ fill in the box

▶ mention one thing

▶ mention a number of things.

As with the Reading paper, there are about **six** different types of questions in the General paper but nearly all the Credit paper questions are either 'mention one thing' or 'mention a number of things'.

This chapter offers you a way to approach the Listening questions and, like Chapter 3 The Reading Paper, works through examples from Past Papers and provides extra examples for you to try on your own. When you see this symbol, it means that audio files are available online, at www.brightredpublishing.co.uk. The transcripts for these recordings are printed at the back of the book. It is highly recommended that you do not read them until after you have worked through the exam questions, listening to the audio files.

Although refining your exam technique is important, your best preparation for the Listening paper is to listen to as much French as possible. You must also revise your vocabulary regularly. Make sure you learn **all** the vocabulary included in Chapter 7 of this book!

Listening practice

The more you listen to French, the more your ear becomes tuned to the sound of the language. Listen to French throughout your *Standard Grade French* course, not just on the lead up to your exam. This way you will get your 'French ear' tuned in well in advance and you will get more out of your French lessons.

The Internet

You can use the Internet to watch French TV shows, news clips and to listen to French radio. As well as being educational, these media sources can be fun and bring you a direct experience of French culture. Try the following links:

http://www.listenlive.eu/france.html

http://www.teachers.tv/video/2261

http://www.tv5.org/

http://www.bbc.co.uk/languages/french

DVDs

Put your favourite DVDs into French and watch them with English subtitles. Even though you will not understand everything you hear, just listening to the sound of the language and picking up a few words will improve your ability to understand spoken French.

Pronunciation

When you are listening to French, be aware that certain sounds will not be written down in the same way that you hear them. Here are some hints about picking up the sounds.

▶ The French often do not pronounce the ends of words, so for example the words *œuf* (egg), *suis* (am) and *habitent* (live) are pronounced 'euh', 'swee' and 'abeet'.

▶ The letters *a* and *e* are often pronounced as an 'o' and words that end –*ns* have an '–ng' pronunciation. For example, *dans* (in) is not pronounced like 'dance' but like 'dong', and *gens* (people) is not pronounced like 'Jen's' but 'jong'.

▶ The sound *é* in French is like the English sound 'ay'. So, *vélo* (bike) sounds like 'vaylo' not 'veelo' and *les* is pronounced 'lay', not like the English word 'less', because the –*s* is the last letter and is not pronounced.

▶ If the accent is the other way around (è) or shaped like a Chinese hat (ê) then the word <u>is</u> pronounced 'e' like the English word 'less'. For example, *mère* is pronounced like you would read it in English 'mere' whilst *bête* (stupid) is pronounced like the English word 'bet'.

▶ –*eux* on the end of words is pronounced '–oo' like 'soup', for example *heureux* (happy) and *dangereux* (dangerous), as the –*x* is not pronounced. Words without the –*x* have the same sound, for example *bleu* (blue), *peu* (a little) and *jeune* (young).

▶ Combinations of letters like *au* and *eau* are pronounced 'oh'. So, if it's nice weather (*il fait beau*), you pronounce *beau* as 'bo'.

▶ The *i* sound is pronounced 'ee' in French. So, *lit* (bed) is not pronounced like the identical word you know in English that means illuminated, but like the name 'Lee'.

▶ Words ending in –*aim* or –*ain* are nasalized which means that you do not pronounce the last letter but make a slight sound through your nose. The vowel sounds are pronounced 'a'. So *pain* is not pronounced like the English word which you feel when someone hits you, but more like 'pa–', *faim* is said 'fa–' and *main* is 'ma–', all with a slight emphasis at the end of the word created through the nose.

▶ Be careful with the words *deux* and *douze* as the pronunciation is slightly different. First of all, the end of *deux* is not normally pronounced except if it is followed by a vowel. For example, *deux ans* creates a **liaison** which makes the pronunciation 'dooz ong'. With *douze* you always pronounce the end of the word but there is a slight difference in the sound. Try putting on an English accent for *douze* and a Scottish accent for *deux*. Imagine saying the word 'book' in a Scottish accent. The pronunciation is the same sound you need for *deux* and if you say 'book' in an English accent, you have the exact sound you need for *douze*. This is very important in your listening exam so make sure that you can differentiate between the two sounds.

▶ *Oi* sounds are pronounced like 'w–'. For example, *voilà* (there is/here is) is said 'vwola'.

▶ The letter *h* is never pronounced in French, even when it is in the middle of a word. So *haricots* (beans) is pronounced 'areeco' and *thé* (tea) is pronounced like the river 'Tay', not like the word 'the' in English.

▶ Two –*ll*– together are pronounced like a 'y'. For example, *fille* (girl) is pronounced 'feey' and *habiller* (to dress) is pronounced 'abeeay'.

▶ The vowel sound *ei* is like the sound in the English word 'bright', so the town Marseille is pronounced 'marsigh' and the verb *réveiller* (to wake) is pronounced like 'revihyay'.

Look out for

The word *femme* is pronounced nasally, and not 'fem' as you would expect. Watch out for this word as it always catches people out!

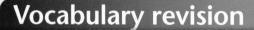

Vocabulary revision

To do well in the Listening paper, revising your vocabulary is absolutely essential. Revising for just 15 minutes every day will help you to retain the vocabulary you have learned. Use the vocabulary lists in Chapter 7 for your revision as these contain most of the words that you need to know. Depending on how much time you have before your exam, you should plan your revision so that you cover every topic.

Vocabulary lists

An active approach is a better aid to memory. Simply reading through vocabulary is not enough. It is better to test yourself on the words each time you learn them and go back over those you find difficult. Here is a good way to do this:

1 Cover the English words with a bookmark, a piece of scrap paper or your hand.

2 For every French word, say the English out loud.

3 Then uncover the word to see if you got it right.

4 If you did, move on the next word. If not, tick the French word in pencil and move on to the next one.

5 At the end of that section, go back and try again to say the words that you ticked.

6 If you get them right this time, rub out the ticks. If you do not, keep going back and trying to say them again. Do not stop until all of the ticks have been rubbed out.

7 Now, go back and cover up the French words. Use the same process to test yourself. You will find this harder but it is well worth the effort because you will remember the vocabulary.

Try this technique with one of the lists from Chapter 7. In the first instance, this activity is best carried out on your own. However, once you have done some revision, it may be helpful to get a friend to test you on the words in a similar way. This enables you to revise the words in a different order and to make sure that you really know them thoroughly.

Recording vocabulary

Another way to revise your vocabulary is to record the words onto tape or MP3 and to listen to them while you are on the go. You can then listen while you are walking to school, tidying your room, playing computer games or doing any activity where you do not need to listen to anything else. Although you will not always be concentrating fully on the words, they will enter your subconscious and you will be amazed at how much you remember. Some people also find it helpful to listen to vocabulary while they are getting to sleep – you will either learn the vocabulary or bore yourself to sleep!

Vocabulary games

To practise the vocabulary that you already know, you could use the websites listed below.

http://www.mflgames.co.uk/

http://www.frenchteacher.net/

http://www.education.vic.gov.au/languagesonline/

http://www.bbc.co.uk/schools/gcsebitesize/french/

The Post-it® note challenge

When it is getting near exam time, you could use Post-it® notes to help you remember the words you have been learning. Why not write down key words, or words that you find difficult to remember, on notes and stick them all over your bedroom (or house if your family will allow it!). You could also draw pictures of the words as this will help you to remember them better and you will recognise the word you have written from a distance. As you get to know the words, you can start to take them down and replace them with new ones.

Try the 'Post-it® note challenge' with words from the Food topic in Chapter 7 Vocabulary. Think about how many words or phrases you can learn in a day. Learning 30 words a day for three days is recommended. This allows you to carry out other revision for French or for other subjects as well, or to carry out your normal routine if you are not on study leave.

Day 1: Write down the first 15 words or phrases and draw pictures where you can. Even if you are not a good artist, the process of attempting the pictures will help you to visualise the word and the silly-looking pictures may also be a source of amusement around the house, cheering you up and relieving your boredom or stress during study time! Stick them in various places where you will see them regularly, for example on the fridge, the bathroom door, the mirror, the TV, your computer. As you get to know the words, replace them with the next 15 words on your list. By about 5pm you should have replaced all of the words so that you can spend the evening revising the new ones.

Day 2: Do the same thing with the next 30 words, that is 15 in the morning and 15 in the evening.

Day 3: Repeat the process.

Day 4: Choose the 20 hardest-to-remember words or phrases from the list and stick these back up all over the house for the whole day.

Day 5: Start all over again with a different set of words.

Word association

When you are learning your vocabulary, write down words that help you to remember each one. You can make up stories about the words to help you remember them. They can be as realistic or silly as you like but the important thing is that they mean something to you. Here are some examples from the topic of 'Daily routine'.

Je me réveille …   I wake up …

Réveille sounds like 'revive' and usually you are revived when you wake up in the morning, or you could think of it as coming back to life. *Je me* sounds like the name 'Jimmy', so you could invent a story about someone called Jimmy who died and came back to life again. Or *réveille* looks and sounds like the confectionery, 'Revels', which gives you a sugar boost and wakes you up.

Je me lève …   I get up …

Lève sounds like 'lever' or 'leave', so either Jimmy is leaving the bed or he is being forced out with a lever.

Je me lave …   I get washed …

Lave sounds like 'laugh' so Jimmy is laughing in the shower.

Je me lave les cheveux.   I wash my hair.

Cheveux vaguely sounds like 'shove you', so Jimmy is laughing because his friends are shoving him into the bathroom to wash his hair.

Je me brosse les dents.   I brush my teeth.

This one's quite easy because *brosse* sounds a bit like 'brush' anyway and *dents* sounds like 'dentures' which you should know are false teeth. So Jimmy is brushing his false teeth.

Je me maquille.   I put on make-up.

Maquille sounds like 'marquee'. Imagine that there was a marquee at a big event specialising in make-up and Jimmy went there to get a make over.

Je me lisse les cheveux.   I straighten my hair.

Lisse sounds like 'release', so you're releasing the straight hair underneath your natural frizz. *Cheveux* sounds a bit like 'shove you', so you're pushing away your unwanted curls and waves.

Je me peigne.   I comb my hair.

Peigne sounds a bit like 'pain', so Jimmy is in pain as he tries to get the tangles out of his hair.

continued

Word association – continued

Je me douche.   I have a shower.

The sound of the water as it comes out of the shower and hits you – doooosh!

Je prends un bain.   I have a bath.

Prends sounds like 'prawn', which is a type of fish that swims in water and *bain* sounds like 'ban'. Prawns are in the sea but, thankfully, they do not appear in the bath so you could think of this as a 'ban on prawns'.

You get the idea. Try doing this with another topic from Chapter 7 Vocabulary. It seems like a lengthy, time-consuming process but actually it saves you time in the long run. You tend to remember the phrases after only going over them a couple of times because you have already done the thinking and memorising while you were making your word associations. Of course, there may be words or phrases which are very difficult to find associations for, but you can simply memorise these words using the cover-and-rub-out-the-ticks technique outlined on page 69.

Mind maps

Once you have a reasonable grasp of your vocabulary, you can revise by creating mind maps of words relating to similar topics. Always use capital letters when you are writing out the words, use lots of different colours for each word or phrase and draw pictures where possible. Let's try that for the topic of Transport.

1 Write the word Transport in the middle of your page, then write all of the possible methods of transport around the word, drawing lines (not arrows) to connect the words together:

2 Now draw lines attached to each of the sub-categories and add additional information to each one. For example, in the train and bus sub-category you could add questions asking for tickets, how much it costs to get to different places, and what time the bus/train leaves. In the plane section, you could put some of the advantages of this form of transport. In the car section, you could write something about how damaging petrol is to the environment. In the boat section, you could write words connected to all the different things that you can do on this method of transport, such as go to restaurants, shops or amusement arcades. You should also remind yourself in the coach section (*car*) that this word does not mean 'car'.

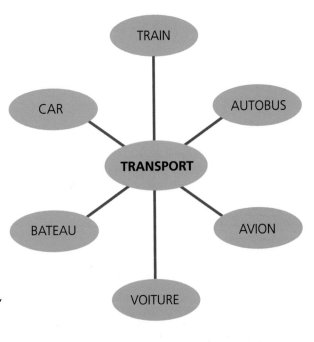

continued

Mind maps – continued

3 There is no limit to how large a mind map can be, so you should draw it on the biggest piece of paper you can. Use A3, if possible, because then you can keep expanding and expanding as you come up with new, related words. For example, once you ask about tickets, you can move on from there to the topic of holidays and what there is to do in different cities and different weather conditions. Constructing your mind map allows you to use the creative side of your brain, which means that you learn lots of information without it seeming like much effort. You are less likely to lose focus and can usually study for much longer periods of time this way – it is just like doodling!

When you use a variety of vocabulary-revision tactics such as the ones described here, wherever you go and whatever you do, you will be coming into contact with important vocabulary. With very little effort at all, you will be subconsciously learning your vocabulary.

À QUELLE HEURE PART LE TRAIN POUR NICE?

MEANS CAR <u>NOT</u> COACH

TRAIN

C'EST COMBIEN POUR ALLER À PARIS?

CAR

AUTOBUS

TRANSPORT

BATEAU

AVION

SUR LE BATEAU ON PEUT:
- MANGER DANS UN RESTAURANT
- VOIR LA MER
- ALLER AUX MAGASINS

VOITURE

LA GASOLINE EST TRÈS MAUVAISE POUR L'AMBIANCE

ALLER EN AVION A BEAUCOUP D'ADVANTAGES:
- C'EST RAPIDE
- C'EST AMUSANT
- ON PEUT VOIR LES NUAGES

Look out for

Keep on going over the words that you have already learned as well as learning new ones. Do not assume that learning them once will keep them in your brain forever!

Checklist of skills for the Listening paper

If you can answer 'Yes' to each of the following skills in the checklist, then you are ready to tackle the Listening paper.

	Checklist	Done
1	I can access useful websites which help me to improve my listening skills.	
2	I know how to revise my vocabulary effectively. (See page 69)	
3	I know how to pronounce key vocabulary in French. (See page 68)	
4	I have learned most of the topic vocabulary lists off by heart. (See Chapter 7)	
5	I can recognise –er, –ir and –re verbs in all tenses. (See Chapter 1)	
6	I can recognise all of the irregular verbs in the present, perfect, future and conditional tenses. (See Chapter 1)	

Complete the sentences in English

There are usually one or two questions of this type in every General Listening paper. The technique for completing these questions is similar to that used for 'Complete the sentences in English' in the Reading paper. Your approach for the Listening is perhaps more active than for the Reading, but the key words still serve as 'place finders'. Additionally, they help to prepare you for listening to the recording. When you listen to the audio file, you will be more tuned in (mentally and aurally) and find it easier to pick out the key words and to concentrate on the answer which follows.

The method for handling this type of question is to:

1 Read the incomplete English sentences carefully. Try to predict the type of answer you need for each one. Use your knowledge of the context given and your imagination. Notice that there are three marks – one mark per correctly completed sentence.

2 Identify the key words before the answers.

3 Translate them into French. Pencil them down if necessary and listen carefully for them in the recording. The answer is likely to come after these words. The recording is played three times.

4 Write down as much of the answer as you can on the first hearing. Try to complete your answer on the second hearing. On the third hearing, check your answer and make sure it is perfect.

Look out for

Remember that you will not have a dictionary in the Listening paper!

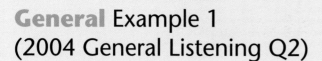

General Example 1
(2004 General Listening Q2)

2. Julie tells you about the plans for tomorrow. What will you be doing?   3
Complete the sentences.

passer   journée
You will be spending the day _____ in town _____.

matin   il y a
In the morning there is a _____ market in the square _____.

centre sportif
In the afternoon, you will go to the sports centre to _____ see my friends _____

_____.

1 Logically, your first answer would either be a place that you might visit or an activity that you would do.

2 The key words are: spend, day.

3 How would you say these words in French? (spend *passer;* day *jour* or *journée*). Pencil these words down if it helps you to remember them. Listen to the audio file and when you hear these words, write down the place or activity that comes after them.

🎧 **Audio file 01**

4 The place was *en ville* (in town). Complete the sentence in English with the answer 'in town'.

The key words for your second sentence are: morning *matin*, there is *il y a*. Now listen.

🎧 **Audio file 02**

After *matin, il y a ...* you heard *marché sur la place*. You should know that *marché* means 'market', but what is *la place?* It looks like the English word 'place' but, in this context, it means something else. Where would you normally hold a market in France? In the square! Sometimes you have to use your common sense. So there is both an activity and a place after the key words. You would complete the sentence with 'a maket in the square'.

For the third sentence, try to think of reasons why you would go to a sports centre. To keep fit? To play football, badminton or tennis? To meet people? Try to anticipate what will be said before you hear it and you will be ready to understand the French more easily. What are the key words this time? (sports centre *centre sportif*). Listen to what is said after these two words.

🎧 **Audio file 03**

What does *voir mes copains* mean? You will know that the word *copains* means 'friends' so, even if you did not pick up the rest, you can assume that the answer is 'to see my friends'.

General Example 2
(2005 General Listening Q7)

Now try this one, using the same approach.

---

7. Julie's father comes home and starts talking to you. What does he tell you?   *Marks*
   Complete the sentences.   **3**

   In 1990 he came to Scotland _____.

   They did a house exchange because _____

   _____.

   He comes back to Scotland _____

   for rugby matches and for holidays.

How might the first sentence be completed? Use your imagination to predict a likely reason why Julie's father may have gone to Scotland. Would he have gone to see a friend, on business, on holiday or for the first time? Your key word is 'Scotland' *Écosse*.

🎧 **Audio file 04**

The answer is 'for the first time'.

For the second sentence, why might people do a house exchange when travelling abroad? What might be the benefits of doing this? Would they be hoping to experience the life of someone in that country, save money, have more independence than they would in a hotel or hostel? Your key words are: house exchange *échange de maisons*. Even if you do not know the word for 'exchange', you do know the word for 'house' *maison*. You will recognise *échange* when you hear it.

🎧 **Audio file 05**

The reason for the house exchange was 'they didn't have much money'.

For the third sentence, you could guess that the answer involves a period of time. The key words are: come back *retourner*, Scotland *Écosse*.

🎧 **Audio file 06**

Your answer is 'every two years'.

General Example 3
(2003 General Listening Q4)

Try this example by yourself.

---

4. Marie tells you about a part-time job she has.

   What does she say? Complete the sentences. **3**

   Marie works in a _____. She helps the customers to

   _____ and she also _____.

 Audio file 07

General Example 4
(2007 General Listening Q13)

---

13. One of the entertainment team at the campsite speaks to you and Jérôme. What does she tell you? Complete the sentences. **3**

   The entertainment team is inviting teenagers to a _____

   this evening at 8.30 pm. Come along and meet _____

   at the site and find out about _____.

 Audio file 08

When you read each question, note how many marks it is worth.

Tick True or False

Usually, there is one True or False question each year in the General Listening paper. Your method for these questions is similar to 'Complete the sentences in English' (see page 74). In a similar way, identifying the key words and trying to think of the corresponding French word will help you to prepare for the recording so that you will be 'tuned in' and can make the most of what you hear. However, rather than acting as 'place finders', the purpose of these keywords is to test the truth of the statements.

As for the Reading, you absolutely must answer this question, even if you have to guess. You have a 50 per cent chance of getting it right! However, using the method given, if you are at all unsure of the sense of what you hear, the presence of all (or most) of the keywords will help to confirm whether or not the statements are true.

General Example 1
(2005 General Listening Q10)

Read the statements carefully.

10. He suggests that you visit the castle of Chambord. Are the statements below **True** or **False**? Tick (✔) the correct boxes. 3

	True	False
situé parc It's situated in a park.		✓
plus grand château région Its the largest castle in the area.	✓	
cheminée chaque jour an, année There is a chimney for every day of the year.	✓	

1 Think about which words you will need to listen for on the audio file.

2 The first sentence states that the castle is in a park. Your key words are: situated, park.

3 In French these words are: siutated *situé*, park *parc*.

4 When more of the key words are present in the recording, it is an indication that the statement is likely to be True. If you hear a different place mentioned, then the statement will most definitely be False.

The second sentence states that it is the largest castle in the area. Your key words are: largest *plus grand*, castle *château*, area *zone/région*. If you hear all these words, you can tick the box for True. The third sentence states that there is a chimney for every day of the year. Your key words are: chimney *cheminée*; every *chaque*; day *jour*; year *an/année*. Listen out for them! Play the audio files and answer the questions.

🎧 **Audio file 09**

Look out for

Remember that if you were to hear a negative such as *ne … pas* in the recording, it might indicate that the statement is false.

General Example 2
(2004 General Listening Q7)

Now try this example.

7. Julie tells you about the football stadium.
   Tick (✔) **True** or **False** for each sentence.   3

	True	False
The stadium is in the town centre.		
It holds 50,000 spectators.		
There is a large car park behind the stadium.		

For the first statement, the keywords are: stadium *stade*, town centre *centre ville*. For the second statement, the keywords are: 50,000 *cinquante mille*, spectators *spectateurs*. For the third statement, the keywords are: car *voiture*, behind *derrière*, stadium *stade*.

🎧 **Audio file 10**

General Example 3
(2003 General Listening Q9)

9. He tells you that he is going on holiday to Finland soon.
   What does he say? Write **T** (**True**) or **F** (**False**) in the boxes below.   3

He is leaving in twelve days.	
He is going for six weeks.	
His aunt and uncle are taking him.	

🎧 **Audio file 11**

Tick the box

There is usually one Tick the box question each year in the General Listening paper. Now that you have had some practice with the True or False questions, you should be able to complete the Tick the box questions fairly easily. As with the True or False questions, the method is to read the English statements actively, translating for yourself the key words before listening to the audio file. Identifying the key words helps to engage your mind with the situation described and recalling the French for these helps to 'tune' your ear so that you are prepared for what you hear on the audio file. If you are unsure of what you have heard, the presence of the key words in the recording will help to confirm that the statement is true. So these key words are 'truth testers' rather than 'place finders'.

General Example 1
(2005 General Listening Q2)

2. She tells you about the village she lives in.
   What does she say about it? Tick (✔) **two** boxes.   **2**

loin It's quite far from Nantes.	
petit église It has a small church.	
mairie There is a town hall.	
ne...pas magasins There are no shops.	

1 Read the statements actively. Think about which words you will need to listen out for. Notice that the instructions are to tick only two boxes.

2 For statement 1 your key words are: far *loin*, the town *Nantes*. For statement 2 your key words are: small, church. For statement 3 your key word is: town hall. For statement 4: no, shops.

3 The French for these key words is: (statement 1) far *loin*, the town *Nantes*; (statement 2) small *petit*; church *église*; (statement 3) town hall *mairie*; (statement 4) no *ne...pas*; shops *magasins*.

4 Listen to the audio file and tick the boxes that you think are correct.

🎧 **Audio file 12**

All the key words for statements 2 and 3 were mentioned in the recording but only half the key words for statements 1 and 4 featured. For statement 1, the word *près* was used instead of *loin* so the village is actually near Nantes. For statement 4, the word *plusieurs* was used instead of *ne ... pas*, so there are several shops in the village.

!Look out for

Do not tick more than two boxes as you will lose marks for the one that is incorrect even if you get the other two right.

General Example 2
(2006 General Listening Q2)

> 2. He introduces you to his family. His mother tells you about the campsite. What
> does she say? Tick (✓) **three** boxes.   3
>
> | | |
> |---|---|
> | The campsite is big. | |
> | It's really quiet. | |
> | There are lots of tents. | |
> | There is a lot for the children to do. | |
> | There is a swimming pool. | |
> | There is a football pitch. | |

Think actively about the statements describing the campsite.

Your key words are: (statement 1) campsite *camping*, big *grand*; (statement 2) quiet
tranquille; (statement 3) lots of *beaucoup de*, tents *tentes*; (statement 4) a lot *beaucoup*,
children *enfants*; (statement 5) swimming pool *piscine*; (statement 6) football *football*.

Listen to the recording and tick the three boxes that you think are correct.

🎧 **Audio file 13**

General Example 3
(2003 General Listening Q7)

Think about your key words. Listen to the recording and tick the three correct boxes.

---

7. When you get there you meet Jean-Claude. He introduces himself, and asks you some questions.

What does he ask you? Tick (✔) **three** boxes. 3

When did you arrive?	
Did you arrive yesterday?	
How long are you here for?	
Is this your first visit to France?	
Have you been to this part of France before?	
Do you like this part of France?	

🎧 **Audio file 14**

Fill in the boxes

These types of questions only come up occasionally in the General Listening paper. For these, you need to complete a table with the details given in the recording. Read the questions carefully and bring to mind what you know about the topic or situation mentioned. You will not be able to use the key word strategy here. Instead, you must rely on listening carefully and using your common sense.

General Example 1
(2006 General Listening Q5)

5. He then talks about the jobs he and his wife do. What does he say? Complete the boxes.   4

	Job	Disadvantage
Father	Works in a bakery	Getting up early
Mother	Nurse	Working until 10pm

Try to think about the different jobs and work places that you know and then listen carefully to what is said on the audio file. Find out which jobs are actually mentioned and see if you can pick up what the disadvantages are. If you cannot understand what is said in the extract, you will still be able to use your common sense. For example, if the job was a policeman, what disadvantages might there be? It is a dangerous job, you would have to come into contact with criminals, it may be stressful and there is a lot of paperwork. Make an educated guess for anything you do not know.

🎧 **Audio file 15**

General Example 2
(2006 General Listening Q8)

Now try this one yourself.

8. Antoine tells you about the jobs he and his sister have to do. What does he say? Complete the boxes. **4**

	At Home	At the Campsite
Antoine		
Mireille		

🎧 **Audio file 16**

Mention one thing

Questions asking for specific information are common in both the General and Credit Listening papers. Read the question carefully so that you are tuned in to the situation described. At this point, however, the key word technique really is aural rather than visual. You will need to pick out the essential words directly from what you hear. Your answers need to be clear and concise.

General Example 1
(2005 General Listening Q1)

> You are staying with your French penpal, Julie, in the Loire Valley.
>
> Tu loges chez ta correspondante française, Julie, dans la vallée de la Loire.
>
> **1.** You have just arrived. What does Julie ask you? **1**
>
> _____

1 Think about the sort of things you would ask someone if they had just arrived in your country. Now listen to the recording.

🎧 **Audio file 17**

2 You need to pick up your key word (or words) aurally. The important word to hear is *manger* (to eat).

3 What question did Julie ask her penpal?

4 The answer is 'Do you want something to eat?'

Credit Example 2
(2003 Credit Listening Q4)

Here is a question from a Credit paper.

---

4.   (a)   Why are Richard's parents sometimes concerned about him?   **2**

   _____

   _____

---

1   Try to think of reasons why parents might be concerned about a teenage boy. What makes your parents worry about you? Now, listen to the recording.

🎧 **Audio file 18**

2   This recording is longer than the previous example from the General paper but you can tackle it in the same way. You cannot really predict the key words in advance. You need to pick them out directly from the French that you hear. The key words you must understand are: *contact, gens, mon* and *âge*.

3   *Contact* and *âge* mean the same as the English. You should know that *gens* means 'people' and *mon* means 'my'. Can you make a sentence with these words? He doesn't have much contact with people his own age.

4   This is the information that you need for your answer. Do not try to add anything else or make any guesses because this will answer the question fully.

Credit Example 3
(2006 Credit Listening Q1)

Try this Credit example on your own.

> You are spending your holidays with your family in a hotel in France.
>
> Tu passes les vacances avec ta famille dans un hôtel en France.
>
> 1. You meet a French boy called Georges who introduces you to his twin sister, Nicole. What does he say? **1**
>
> _____
>
> _____

 Audio file 19

Mention a number of things

Questions asking you to mention a number of things make up about 30 per cent of the Credit Listening papers but are rarely seen in the General Listening. You can use the same skills to answer these questions, but this time you need to ensure that you give the correct amount of information for the marks available. For example, if the question is worth two marks, then you need to give two pieces of information; if it is worth three marks, then you should mention three things. Do not give more or less information than required or you may lose marks. Do not give additional information that you are unsure of as you may lose marks if it is wrong.

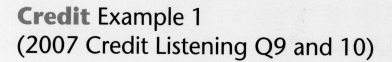

Credit Example 1
(2007 Credit Listening Q9 and 10)

---

9. What does Jacques say about his links with Scotland?   Mention any **two** things.   **2**

He has lived in Scotland for three years.

He has just bought a new house on the west coast.

*   *   *   *   *

10. What difficulties did he have when he first arrived? Mention **two** things.   **2**

---

1 Read question 9 carefully and try to imagine what Jacques' links with Scotland could be. Does he have friends or family there? Does he visit the country often? Has he ever lived there? Does he have Scottish ancestors? Try to predict the type of information you are going to hear.

2 Listen to the file and pick out **two** pieces of information. Notice that there are two marks: one mark per piece of information.

🎧 **Audio file 20**

3 Jacques mentions three points but you only need to write down two. In the first phrase, the key words are: _trois ans_ three years, _j'habite_ I live, _Écosse_ Scotland. In the second part of the sentence, the key words are: _viens d'_ from _venir de_ (to have just...), _acheter_ buy, _nouvelle_ new, _maison_ house, _côte_ coast. In Jacques' final point, the key words are: _amis_ friends, _là-bas_ over there.

4 Your answers are any two of the following:

He has lived in Scotland for three years.

He has just bought a new house on the west coast.

He and his wife have good friends over there.

Now read question 10. Try to put yourself in Jacques' situation. What kind of difficulties might you face when you go to another country for the first time? Might you have difficulties with the language? Would you know anyone? Would you be able to find work? Listen carefully to the audio file and try to pick out the two problems that Jacques mentions.

🎧 **Audio file 21**

This time, Jacques mentions only two points so you have to understand everything. In the first sentence, the key words are: _connaissais_ from the verb _connaître_ (to know), _personne_ no-one. So you can deduce from this that Jacques did not know anyone. In the second sentence, the key words are: _comprendre_ to understand, _Écossais_ Scottish, _accent_ accent. You should write that he finds it hard to understand Scottish people because of their accents.

Credit Example 2
(2006 Credit Listening Q2–4)

2. Georges' mother tells you about their holidays. What does she say? Mention any **two** things.   2

_____

_____

    *   *   *   *   *

3. She then explains what there is to do in the area. What does she say? Mention any **two** things.   2

_____

_____

    *   *   *   *   *

4. Georges talks about his sporting activities. What does he tell you? Mention any **two** things.   2

_____

_____

Read question 2 and think about what you would say about your holidays. Georges' mother will probably say where they go, where they stay, how long they go for, and so on. Listen carefully to the recording.

🎧 **Audio file 22**

Georges' mother has given three pieces of information, but you only need to mention two of them. The key words for the first sentence are: *semaine* week, *juillet* July, *mari* husband, *travailler* work. They only spend a week in July because her husband has to work.

In the second sentence, the key words are: *vacances* holidays, *principales* main, *hiver* winter. For them, the main holidays are in winter. The key words for the last sentence are: *passons* spend, *quinzaine* fortnight, *ski* ski, *Suisse* Switzerland. They spend a fortnight skiing in Switzerland.

Now try questions 3 and 4 on your own. For question 3 you need to write down two points. Listen carefully.

🎧 **Audio file 23**

What might Georges say about sporting events? Write down two points.

🎧 **Audio file 24**

Summary

▸ Always read the introductions to the questions.

▸ Read the questions carefully before you begin listening to the audio files.

▸ Use the marks available as a guide to how much to write.

▸ Try to predict the type of answers you are likely to hear.

▸ Listen carefully for key words in the passage.

▸ Write down as much as you can on the first hearing.

▸ Try to complete your answers on the second hearing, and on the third hearing check your answer and make sure it's perfect.

▸ Check all of your answers at the end and confirm that everything makes sense.

▸ Fill in any blanks with 'educated guesses'.

You will produce several Folio essays in class and must choose three of these essays for your final grade. These essays should be on different topics, each about 150 words in length and use a variety of structures. To achieve the best grade possible for your essays, you will need to study Chapter 1 Language skills very carefully to learn how to use verbs properly, write in different tenses and put sentences together accurately.

How to write a good Folio essay

Choosing a good topic

Choose topics which allow you to express your ideas fully and, if possible, make use of at least two different tenses. For example, in an essay on 'Holidays' you could write about a holiday you have been on (past tense), the sort of holidays you like to go on (present tense) and where you would like to go in the future (future or conditional tenses), but an essay on 'Daily Routine' would only allow you to write in the present tense, unless you are very inventive!

Developing ideas and varying sentence structure

You must develop the ideas in your essay fully, using complex sentences and varying the structures that you use. For example, instead of writing: *Je suis allé(e) à Paris. Je suis allé(e) en autobus. Je suis allé(e) à la tour Eiffel. C'était bien!* (I went to Paris. I went by bus. I went to the Eiffel Tower. It was good!), you might write: *Je suis allé(e) à Paris avec un groupe scolaire. Nous avons voyagé en autobus et pendant le voyage j'ai visité la tour Eiffel ce qui était intéressant parce que c'était très grande et il y avait beaucoup de monde là!* (I went to Paris with a school group. We travelled by bus and during the journey I visited the Eiffel Tower which was interesting because it was very big and there were lots of people there.) Both of these examples give the same information but the second example includes much more detail and joins the sentences together with a variety of conjunctions (*et, parce que* and *ce qui*).

Look out for

Did you notice the way the opinion was expressed in the second example? *Ce qui était très intéressant!* The expression, *ce qui* (which) is very useful because it helps you to make complex sentences without too much effort and, combined with other key features, allows you to get that all-important Credit grade.

Complex sentences

It is essential to build on your sentences and to go beyond giving only the basic information to gain the best mark that you can. Think of it as Lego® – you are joining more and more pieces on to your basic sentence. For example:

1 *Je vais au cinéma*. I go to the cinema.

2 *Le vendredi soir, je vais au cinéma avec mes amis*. On Friday night, I go to the cinema with my friends.

3 *Normalement, le vendredi soir, si j'ai de l'argent, je vais au cinéma avec mes amis à Édimbourg parce que j'adore regarder les films et ça m'amuse beaucoup*. Normally, on Friday nights, if I have money, I go to the cinema with my friends in Edinburgh because I love watching films and I enjoy it a lot.

Varying sentence structure

Avoid starting too many sentences with *je* because this makes the language seem limited and unimaginative. If you are describing things that you do with other people, alternate between using *je* (I), *nous* (we) and *on* (we) so as not to be repetitive.

Use time expressions to begin sentences, like *le week-end* (at the weekend), *l'année dernière* (last year), *souvent* (often), *quelquefois* (sometimes).

Rephrase some of your sentences so that they begin with a different word. For example:

▶ *J'aime le foot*. ▶ *Le foot me plaît*. (I like football)

▶ *Je vais au collège en voiture* ▶ *Ma mère me conduit au collège*. (I go to school by car. ▶ My mum drives me to school.)

▶ *Je voudrais devenir coiffeur*. ▶ *Mon rêve est de devenir coiffeur*. (I would like to become a hairdresser. ▶ My dream is to become a hairdresser.)

▶ *Je suis allé(e) en vacances avec ma famille*. ▶ *Ma famille et moi, nous sommes partis en vacances*. (I went on holiday with my family. ▶ My family and I went on holiday together.)

▶ *Je fais de la natation tous les mardis*. ▶ *Tous les mardis je fais de la natation*. (I go swimming every Tuesday. ▶ Every Tuesday I go swimming.)

▶ *J'étudie les maths et les sciences*. ▶ *Mes matières sont les maths et les sciences*. (I study maths and science. ▶ My subjects are maths and science.)

▶ *J'adore faire du théâtre*. ▶ *Faire du théâtre c'est ma passion*. (I love acting. ▶ Acting is my passion.)

Giving opinions and using synonyms

To achieve a good grade, it is essential to give your opinions but it is also important to introduce them in a variety of ways. Avoid overusing the phrase *c'était* + adjective. *C'était bien, c'était super, c'était marrant* is too repetitive. Instead, you could use some of the following phrases:

D'après moi ..., Selon moi ..., À mon avis ...   In my opinion ...

Je pense que ..., Je crois que ..., J'estime que ... I think ...

Çela me paraît ..., Il me semble ..., Pour ma part ...   It seems to me ...

As often as possible, give reasons for your opinions. Ensure that you vary the way you introduce these reasons – avoid using *parce que* (because) all the time. Here are some other phrases which could be used:

parce que ...	**because ...**
car ...	because ...
étant donné que ...	given that ...
puisque ...	since, seeing that ...
vu que ...	in view of the fact that ..., considering that ...

Another word which is often overused in Folio essays is *mais* (but). There are lots of variations on this word. Make sure you use them!

mais ...	**but**
cependant ...	nevertheless, however, yet
néanmoins ...	nevertheless, yet
pourtant ...	nevertheless, even so, all the same
toutefois ...	however

To make your essay a bit more sophisticated, here are a variety of words that you could use instead of *aussi* (also):

aussi	**also**
à cela s'ajoute ...	add to that, in addition to
d'ailleurs ...	besides, moreover
de/en plus ...	further more
en outre ...	besides, moreover
par ailleurs ...	in other respects

Structuring your essay

Ensure that your essay has a clear beginning, middle and end. Each sentence and paragraph should lead into the next, so that your ideas develop naturally within an organised framework.

Here is a sample essay.

Les vacances

J'adore les vacances! L'année dernière je suis allée en France avec ma famille ce qui était super! Nous allions à la plage tous les jours et je me faisais beaucoup bronzer. Je suis restée en France pendant quinze jours et nous avons voyagé en voiture et en bateau. J'aime bien les bateaux parce qu'on peut voir la mer. En plus, nous avons logé dans un grand appartement avec trois chambres, une petite cuisine et une salle de bains. Il y avait aussi un balcon ce qui m'a plu. Il faisait beau la plupart du temps mais quelquefois il pleuvait. Les soirs j'allais en discothèque avec ma sœur et nous dansions toutes les nuits. C'était amusant car la musique française est très différente de la musique d'ici!

L'année prochaine je voudrais aller en Espagne avec mes amis, peut-être à Madrid ou à Barcelone puisqu'il y a beaucoup de musées intéressants là-bas. Je voyagerais en avion, je visiterais tous les monuments historiques et je ferais des achats au grand centre commercial qui s'appelle El Corte Inglés. Je mangerais la nourriture traditionnelle de la région comme l'omelette espagnole, la paella et du poisson et je logerais dans un hôtel de cinq étoiles. Je meurs d'envie d'y aller. Ça c'est mon rêve!

224 words

Grade 1

Look out for

Make sure that your essays are the correct length and not too short to qualify for a Credit grade.

Translation

I love holidays! Last year, I went to France with my family, which was fantastic. We went to the beach every day and I sunbathed a lot. I stayed in France for two weeks and we travelled by car and by boat. I really like boats because you can see the sea. As well as that, we stayed in a big flat with three bedrooms, a little kitchen and a bathroom. There was also a balcony which I liked. The weather was nice most of the time but sometimes it rained. In the evenings I went to the disco with my sister and we danced every night. It was fun because French music is very different from the music here!

Next year I would like to go to Spain with my friends, perhaps to Madrid or to Barcelona since there are lots of interesting museums there. I would travel by plane, visit all the historical monuments and go shopping at the big shopping centre, called the Corte Inglés. I would eat traditional food from the region like Spanish omelette, paella and fish and I would stay in a 5-star hotel. I can't wait to go there. That's my dream.

continued

...sure that your essays are the correct length and not too short to qualify for a Credit grade.

- The opening statement introduces the theme of the essay.
- The first paragraph is all about a holiday in the past whereas the second paragraph is about a holiday the candidate would like to go on.

- Conjunctions like *ce qui, et, en plus, puisque, car, peut-être* and *parce que* are used to join sentences so that the essay can flow well.
- The last sentence concludes the essay well as it gives an opinion and summarises what has been said throughout the second paragraph.
- The essay is slightly longer than the recommended 150 words. This can be beneficial, as it allows you to show the examiner the depth of your writing skills and to use a greater variety of tenses and structures. However, short and accurate is better than long and full of mistakes.

Look out for

When you are referring to countries and cities make sure that you have used *en* and *à* correctly. Use *à* before cities, for example *à Paris, à Londres*. Names of cities that include the article become *au*, for example 'to Le Havre' is *au Havre*. Use *en* (in) before continents, feminine countries and masculine singular countries starting with a vowel, for example *en France, en Allemagne, en Iran*. Use *aux/au* before plural countries, and masculine singular countries starting with a consonant, for example *aux États-Unis, au Canada, au Portugal, au Maroc, au Japon, au pays de Galles*.

Accuracy

Your essay must be accurate to do well in *Standard Grade French*. To achieve this, ensure that you:

- use Chapter 1 Language skills carefully when conjugating verbs
- remember to check your spelling, adjective agreements and put accents on where necessary
- make use of the vocabulary that you have been given in class to prepare the essays
- use Chapter 2 Dictionary skills to help you to get the correct meaning in French for the English word that you are looking for
- check your teacher's corrections carefully and redraft your essays accurately
- memorise your redrafted work thoroughly before your assessment, making sure that you do not miss out any words or put the accents on the wrong way round.

How to prepare for the Folio assessment

You will have 30 minutes to write your essay under exam conditions in class with no notes and only a dictionary to help you. Therefore, once you have prepared your essay and it has been corrected and redrafted, it is advisable to memorise it. The techniques for committing your essay to memory are similar to those used for vocabulary revision (see page 69).

Memorising your essay

1 Take a sheet of A4 lined paper and write out each sentence of your essay on a different line, double-spacing them.

2 Look at the first sentence and try to learn it.

3 Practise saying it in your head.

4 Write it down on a separate piece of paper without looking at it.

5 Check that you got it right and that the spelling was accurate. If not, try again.

6 When you can write the sentence accurately, repeat the process for the next sentence. This time you need to remember both sentences.

7 Continue doing this with every sentence, each time writing more and more sentences down at a time. By the end, you will have written out your whole essay without looking.

8 Leave your essay for a couple of hours, then go back and see if you can still remember it. If not, go through the same steps again until you can.

9 Try again the next day. If you can still remember your essay without looking, then you are ready for your assessment.

You may find it easier to split your essay up into parts, learning a few sentences each day. Make sure you allow yourself time to do this.

You may also find it helpful to record yourself saying your essay onto a sound file and putting this onto your iPod®. This way, you can listen to your essay on your way to school, in your bedroom and as you are drifting off to sleep. Your subconscious will take in the information even when you are not fully concentrating on trying to learn it.

Finally, you could ask someone to help you learn your essay by getting them to read out parts of your essay to you and repeating what they say until you can eventually say the entire essay to them without looking. They can check that you say exactly what is on the paper and they can jog your memory if you get stuck or remind you of any parts that you have missed out.

Summary

▶ Choose a good topic for your essay.
▶ Conjugate your verbs accurately.
▶ Vary the words and phrases that you use.
▶ Use joining words to link your sentences together.
▶ Give opinions.
▶ Make sure that your essay is the right length.
▶ Get your essay corrected and learn it well in advance of your assessment.
▶ Memorise your work.

complete three different types of
assessments: a presentation, a discussion
a role-play. It is worth spending a long time
preparing for these assessments as the overall
Speaking grade counts for 33 per cent of your final
exam – this can have a huge effect on your overall
grade. The Speaking assessments are also one of
the easiest ways to boost your grades because you
can get all the help you need in class from your
teacher when you are preparing them, you can use
a dictionary and you can get the teacher to correct
what you intend to say before the assessment. All
you need to do then is to learn the main points
and a few phrases to join it together!

The presentation

The presentation is the most straightforward assessment as you can use the same
topic as one of your Folio essays. Of course, you may need to adjust your essay
so that it sounds more like a spoken presentation, but your basic piece of work is
already done for you.

Your presentation should last between one and two minutes and you will be allowed
five headings of up to eight words each in French or in English. Depending on how
confident you are about being spontaneous, you may prefer to prepare by learning
just the outline of your presentation, rather than memorising it word for word, as
this will sound more natural. However, if necessary, you can use the same technique
to memorise it as described in Chapter 5 The Folio (Writing).

To achieve a Credit grade for the presentation, you must:

❱ give a full and comprehensive presentation

❱ speak accurately using varied structures

❱ give opinions and support them with reasons

❱ be able to pronounce the words correctly.

The discussion

The discussion should last between two and five minutes and will be on a topic you have agreed with your teacher. To get a Grade 1 or 2 for this assessment, you must:

▶ understand all the questions you are asked straight away

▶ give opinions and reasons

▶ respond accurately to additional questions

▶ speak fluently and be accurate with your grammar and pronunciation

▶ use a range of structures to express yourself.

You are not allowed to take in any notes for this assessment.

It is possible to do the discussion on the same topic as your presentation, and many candidates find this an easier option. Your teacher will ask you questions about the topic in French and, if you are to achieve a Credit grade, you will need to give detailed, accurate answers.

1 To prepare for this assessment, you should write down all the questions that you could possibly be asked. If the discussion is on the same topic as your presentation, bear in mind the information you have already given.

2 You should then put the questions into French and start preparing your answers.

3 Make sure you get your teacher to correct your preparation material before you start to learn it.

4 You can then begin memorising it using the technique described in Chapter 5 The Folio (Writing). This time, however, you are learning questions rather than sentences.

Look out for

You will need to learn the possible questions or you may not understand what your teacher has asked you!

Look out for

You can gain Brownie points by preparing a couple of questions to ask your teacher on the agreed topic.

Phrases to avoid gaps & hesitations

Cela m'interésse beaucoup …	This really interests me …
Je me passionne pour ce thème …	I'm passionate about this issue …
J'ai beaucoup à dire à ce sujet, par exemple …	I've got a lot to say on this subject, for example …
Je ne veux pas trop dire …	I don't want to say too much …
C'est une question intéressante, difficile à répondre.	That's an interesting question, difficult to answer.
Je suis d'accord avec … qui dit que …	I agree with … who says that …
par contre	on the other hand
autrement dit	in other words
Pouvez-vous répéter la question, s'il vous plaît?	Can you repeat the question please?
Désolé(e), mais j'ai oublié ma réponse à cette question.	Sorry, but I've forgotten my answer to this question.
J'aimerais bien répondre à votre question mais je préfère ne pas parler de ce sujet.	I would really like to answer your question but I prefer not to talk about this subject.
Comme j'ai déjà dit …	As I've already said …
Je ne sais pas.	I don't know.
Je n'ai aucune idée.	I've no idea.

The role-play

The role-play gives you the opportunity to work with your peers and, for this reason, it is usually popular. For this assessment, you will be given a scenario where you need to use polite language to obtain or provide a service. For example, you may have to book a holiday with a travel agent, buy something in a clothes shop or explain what is wrong with you at the doctor's. A friend or classmate plays the part of the person providing the service and the conversation should last between two and five minutes. To achieve a top mark for this assessment, you should follow the same criteria as for the discussion (see page 99). Like the discussion, you will not be allowed any notes for this part of the assessment.

1 For this assessment, you should prepare your dialogue with your partner so that you both understand what you have to say. Make it as imaginative as possible.

2 Ensure that you always use the *vous* form as it is a formal situation and try to use longer, more complex sentences where possible.

3 Get your teacher to correct your work when you have finished (before you begin to learn it).

4 For this type of assessment, you may find it more helpful to work on learning the role-play together, rather than individually, as you also need to remember what your partner has to say (so that you know when to come in with your part). Of course, if you feel confident, you can also be spontaneous and bring in new material if it is relevant to the role-play to make it sound more natural.

Summary

▶ Prepare your presentation well in advance.

▶ Vary your sentence structures and give opinions.

▶ Ensure your presentation lasts for the right length of time.

▶ Learn the main points from your presentation thoroughly.

▶ Try to pronounce your words as accurately as possible with the best French accent you can manage.

▶ Prepare for every question your teacher could possibly ask.

▶ Be prepared to ask your teacher some questions too.

▶ Learn some extra phrases to fill in the gaps if you forget or do not know what to say.

chapter has been grouped by topic. If you can learn all these words off by heart, you ... ...ell in your exam. For various ways to memorise lists of vocabulary, see Chapter 4 The Listening ...es 66–91).

Personal information

Bonjour! — **Hello!**
Ça va? — How are you?
Ça va très bien! — Very well!
Ça va super! — I'm great.
Comme ci comme ça. — So so.
Ça va mal. — I'm ill.
Ça va pas très bien. — I'm not very well.
Et toi? — And you?
Merci! — Thank you!
Au revoir! — Goodbye!

Comment t'appelles-tu? — **What is your name?**
Je m'appelle … — I'm called …
Mon nom est … — My name is …

Quel âge as-tu? — **How old are you?**
J'ai … ans. — I'm … years old.

Où habites-tu? — **Where do you live?**
J'habite à Édimbourg. — I live in Edinburgh.
J'habite en Écosse. — I live in Scotland.
J'habite en France. — I live in France.
J'habite en Angleterre. — I live in England.
J'habite en Allemagne. — I live in Germany.
J'habite en Italie. — I live in Italy.
J'habite en Espagne. — I live in Spain.
J'habite au pays de Galles. — I live in Wales.
J'habite au Luxembourg. — I live in Luxembourg.

Tu es de quelle nationalité? — **What nationality are you?**
Je suis écossais(e). — I'm Scottish.
Je suis anglais(e). — I'm English.
Je suis britannique. — I'm British.
Je suis français(e). — I'm French.
Je suis italien(ne). — I'm Italian.
Je suis espagnol(e). — I'm Spanish.
Je suis allemand(e). — I'm German.
Je suis belge. — I'm Belgian.
Je suis gallois(e). — I'm Welsh.
Je suis luxembourgeois(e). — I'm a Luxembourger.

As-tu des frères et des sœurs? — **Do you have brothers and sisters?**
J'ai un frère. — I have a brother.
J'ai une sœur. — I have one sister.
J'ai deux frères et deux sœurs. — I have two brothers and two sisters.
Je n'ai pas de frères ou de sœurs. — I don't have any brothers or sisters.
Je n'ai ni frère ni sœur. — I have neither brother nor sister.

Je suis fils/fille unique. — I'm an only child.
J'ai un demi-frère. — I have a half-brother.
J'ai une demi-sœur. — I have a half-sister.

Comment s'appelle ta mère? — **What is your mum called?**
Ma mère s'appelle … — My mum is called …
Comment s'appelle ton père? — What is your dad called?
Mon père s'appelle … — My dad is called …
Comment s'appellent tes parents? — What are your parents called?

J'ai un frère … — **I have a brother …**
qui s'appelle … — who is called …
J'ai deux sœurs — I have two sisters
qui s'appellent … — who are called …

ma famille — **my family**
mon père — my father
ma mère — my mother
mon frère — my brother
ma sœur — my sister
mon beau-père — my step-father/father-in-law
ma belle-mère — my step-mother/mother-in-law

mon demi-frère — my half-brother
ma demi-sœur — my half sister
mon frère jumeau — my twin-brother
ma sœur jumelle — my twin-sister
mon cousin/ma cousine — my cousin

mon oncle	my uncle	*un chat*	a cat
ma tante	my aunt	*un cheval*	a horse
mon copain	my friend	*un chien*	a dog
ma copine	my friend	*un hamster*	a hamster
mon petit-ami	my boyfriend	*un lapin*	a rabbit
ma petite-amie	my girlfriend	*un oiseau*	a bird
		un poisson	a fish
As-tu un animal?	**Have you got a pet?**	*un poisson rouge*	a goldfish
Je n'ai pas d'animal.	I haven't got a pet.	*une souris*	a mouse
J'ai …	I've got …		

Descriptions

Tu es comment?	**What are you like?**
J'ai …	I have …
les yeux bleus	blue eyes
les yeux marrons	brown eyes
les yeux verts	green eyes
les yeux noisette	hazel eyes
les cheveux blonds	blond hair
les cheveux bruns	brown hair
les cheveux noirs	black hair
les cheveux roux	red hair
les cheveux châtains	chestnut hair
les cheveux longs	long
les cheveux courts	short
les cheveux mi-longs	mid-length
les cheveux bouclés, frisés	curly
les cheveux raides	straight

Je suis …	**I am …**
assez	quite
très	very
grand(e)	tall
petit(e)	small
de taille moyenne	of medium height
bavard(e)	talkative
gourmand(e)	greedy
ennuyeux(–euse)	boring

marrant(e)	fun/funny
paresseux(–euse)	lazy
sportif(–ve)	sporty, athletic
timide	shy

Je porte des lunettes.	**I wear glasses.**
Je porte des lentilles de contact.	I wear contact lenses.

Numbers

0	*zéro*	11	*onze*
1	*un/une*	12	*douze*
2	*deux*	13	*treize*
3	*trois*	14	*quatorze*
4	*quatre*	15	*quinze*
5	*cinq*	16	*seize*
6	*six*	17	*dix-sept*
7	*sept*	18	*dix-huit*
8	*huit*	19	*dix-neuf*
9	*neuf*	20	*vingt*
10	*dix*		

Speech: BAAA BAAA / Soixante-dix-neuf …

		51	cinquante-et-un	81	quatre-vingt-un
		52	cinquante-deux	82	quatre-vingt-deux
		53	cinquante-trois	83	quatre-vingt-trois
		54	cinquante-quatre	84	quatre-vingt-quatre
	vingt-cinq	55	cinquante-cinq	85	quatre-vingt-cinq
	vingt-six	56	cinquante-six	86	quatre-vingt-six
	vingt-sept	57	cinquante-sept	87	quatre-vingt-sept
28	vingt-huit	58	cinquante-huit	88	quatre-vingt-huit
29	vingt-neuf	59	cinquante-neuf	89	quatre-vingt-neuf
30	trente	60	soixante	90	quatre-vingt-dix
31	trente-et-un	61	soixante-et-un	91	quatre-vingt-onze
32	trente-deux	62	soixante-deux	92	quatre-vingt-douze
33	trente-trois	63	soixante-trois	93	quatre-vingt-treize
34	trente-quatre	64	soixante-quatre	94	quatre-vingt-quatorze
35	trente-cinq	65	soixante-cinq	95	quatre-vingt-quinze
36	trente-six	66	soixante-six	96	quatre-vingt-seize
37	trente-sept	67	soixante-sept	97	quatre-vingt-dix-sept
38	trente-huit	68	soixante-huit	98	quatre-vingt-dix-huit
39	trente-neuf	69	soixante-neuf	99	quatre-vingt-dix-neuf
40	quarante			100	cent
		70	soixante-dix		
41	quarante-et-un	71	soixante-et-onze	1000	mille
42	quarante-deux	72	soixante-douze	1 000 000	un million
43	quarante-trois	73	soixante-treize		
44	quarante-quatre	74	soixante-quatorze		
45	quarante-cinq	75	soixante-quinze		
46	quarante-six	76	soixante-seize		
47	quarante-sept	77	soixante-dix-sept		
48	quarante-huit	78	soixante-dix-huit		
49	quarante-neuf	79	soixante-dix-neuf		
50	cinquante	80	quatre-vingts		

Daily routine

Qu'est-ce que tu fais le matin?	What do you do in the morning?
Je me réveille …	I wake up …
Je me lève …	I get up …
Je me lave …	I get dressed …
Je me lave les cheveux.	I wash my hair.
Je me brosse les dents.	I brush my teeth.
Je me maquille.	I put on make-up.
Je me lisse les cheveux.	I straighten my hair.
Je me peigne.	I comb my hair.
Je me douche.	I have a shower.
Je prends un bain.	I have a bath.
Je prends le petit déjeuner.	I have breakfast.
Je mange …	I eat …
des céréales	cereal
du pain grillé	toast
Je quitte la maison …	I leave the house …
Je vais au collège …	I go to school …
J'arrive au collège …	I arrive at school …
Je travaille en classe.	I work in class.

Et l'après-midi?	And in the afternoon?	À quelle heure?	At what time?
Je mange à la cantine.	I eat in the cafeteria.	*à sept heures*	at 7:00
Je vais aux cours.	I go to class.	*à sept heures dix*	at 7:10
Je joue au foot.	I play football.	*à sept heures et quart*	at 7:15
Je parle avec mes copains.	I talk to my friends.	*à sept heures vingt*	at 7:20
Je rentre chez moi.	I go home.	*à sept heures et demie*	et 7:30
		à huit heures moins vingt	at 7:40
		à huit heures moins le quart	at 7:45
Et le soir?	**And in the evening?**	*à huit heures mons dix*	at 7:50
Je regarde la télé.	I watch TV.		
J'écoute de la musique.	I listen to music.		
Je fais mes devoirs.	I do my homework.		
Je sors …	I go out …		
Je promène le chien.	I walk the dog.		
Je dîne …	I have dinner …		
Je range mes affaires.	I tidy my things.		
Je lis …	I read …		
Je joue à l'ordinateur.	I play on the computer.		
Je me couche …	I go to bed …		
Je dors.	I sleep.		

Clothes and shopping

Qu'est-ce que tu portes?	What are you wearing?
Je porte …	I am wearing/I wear …
un sweat, un pull	a jumper
un jean	jeans
un manteau	a coat
un pantalon	trousers
un tee-shirt	a T-shirt
un chemisier	a blouse
une chemise	a shirt
une cravate	a tie
une écharpe	a scarf
une jupe	a skirt
une robe	a dress
une veste	a jacket
des gants	gloves
des baskets	trainers
des bottes	boots
des chaussures	shoes
des chaussettes	socks
à carreaux	checked
à rayures	striped
bleu marine	navy blue
bleu clair	light blue
bleu foncé	dark blue

Qu'est-ce qu'il porte?	What is he wearing?
Qu'est-ce qu'elle porte?	What is she wearing?
Je pense que …	I think that …
Je trouve que …	I find that …
Je crois que …	I believe that …
La mode est importante.	Fashion is important.
À mon avis …	In my opinion …
les vêtements	clothes
ne sont pas importants	aren't important

Quand je sors …	When I go out
Je mets …	I put on …
Ma marque préférée c'est …	My favourite make is …
J'adore surtout …	I especially like …
les couleurs	the colours
le style	the style
la qualité	the quality
de ces vêtements	of these clothes
Il y a des gens …	there are people
Qui disent qu' …	who say that
acheter les vêtements …	buying clothes …
c'est une perte …	is a waste …
d'argent	of money
de temps	of time
Je suis d'accord …	I agree …
car je déteste la mode	because I hate fashion
Je ne suis pas d'accord	I don't agree because …
parce que …	

Où habites-tu?	**Where do you live?**
Où habitez-vous?	Where do you live?
J'habite …	I live …
Nous habitons …	We live …
à la campagne	in the country
à la montagne	in the mountains
au bord de la mer	by the sea
dans un village	in a village
en ville	in town
en banlieue	in the suburbs
une ferme	a farm
dans …	in…
un appartement	a flat
un immeuble	a block of flats
une maison	a house
Édimbourg, c'est quelle sorte de ville?	What kind of town is Edinburgh?
Ma ville est …	My town is …
grande	big
moderne	modern
historique	historical
touristique	touristic

Qu'est-ce qu'on peut faire dans ta ville?	**What can you do in your town?**
À Édimbourg il y a …	In Edinburgh there is/are …
Près de chez moi il y a …	Near my house there is/are …
Dans mon quartier il y a …	In my area there is/are …
un aéroport	an airport
un café	a café
un château	a castle
un cinéma	a cinema
un commissariat de police	a police station
une gare	a train station
une église	a church
un supermarché	a supermarket
des magasins	shops
un jardin public	a park
un zoo	a zoo
un lycée	a school
un collège	a school
une école primaire	a primary school
une banque	a bank
une piscine	a swimming pool
une auberge de jeunesse	a youth hostel
une cathédrale	a cathedral
des musées	museums
des restaurants	restaurants

CAFÉ JACQUES

Où vas-tu …	**Where do you go …**
le week-end?	at the weekend?
le soir?	in the evening?
après le collège?	after school?
Je vais …	I go …
au centre ville	to town
au cinéma U.C.I./Odéon	to the U.C.I./Odeon cinema
au bowling	to the bowling alley
chez Burger King	to Burger King
chez McDo	to McDonald's
à la patinoire	to the ice rink
à la disco	to the disco
aux magasins	to the shops

Directions

Excusez-moi ...	**Excuse me ...**
où est ... ?	where is... ?
Où se trouve ... ?	where is... ?
la piscine	the swimming pool
s'il vous plaît	please
à la poste	to the post office
à l'hôpital	to the hospital
à l'hôtel de ville	to the town hall
au stade	to the stadium
Tournez à gauche.	Turn/go left.
Tournez à droite.	Turn/go right.
Allez tout droit.	Go straight ahead.
Prenez ...	Take ...
la première rue ...	the first street ...
à gauche	on the left
la deuxième rue ...	the second street ...
à droite	on the right
C'est à gauche.	It's on the left.
C'est à droite.	It's on the right.

Traversez ...	Cross ...
la place	the square
Passez ...	Go over
le pont	the bridge

Transport and travel

Comment vas-tu ...	**How do you get ...**
en ville	to town
chez tes copains	to your friends' houses
chez tes grands-parents	to your grandparents'
au bord de la mer	to the seaside
en France	to France
au Japon	to Japan
Je vais ...	I go ...
J'y vais ...	I go there ...
à cheval	on horse
à pied	on foot
à moto	by motorbike
en autobus	by bus
en avion	by plane
en bateau	by boat
en car	by coach
en fusée	by rocket
en hélicoptère	by helicopter
en train	by train
en vélo	by bike
en voiture	by car
Je vais en ville en autobus.	I go to town by bus.
Je vais au supermarché à pied.	I go to the supermarket on foot.

… rooms

…maison?	What's your house like?
… écrire ta maison?	Can you describe your house?
Il y a combien de pièces?	How many rooms are there?
Il y a … pièces.	There are … rooms.
au sous-sol	in the basement
au rez-de-chaussée	on the ground floor
au premier/deuxième/ troisième étage	on the first/second/third floor
dans la mansarde	in the attic
Il y a …	There is …
Nous avons …	We have …
le bureau	the study
la chambre	the bedroom
la cuisine	the kitchen
la douche	the shower
l'entrée	the entrance hall
la salle à manger	the dining hall
la salle de bains	the dining room
la salle de jeux	the games room
le salon	the living room
l'escalier	the staircase
un jardin	a garden
un balcon	a balcony
une cave	a cellar
un garage (pour la voiture)	a garage (for the car)

Dans le jardin il y a …	**In the garden there is/ are …**
une pelouse	a lawn
des fleurs	flowers

J'aime bien ma maison …	**I really like my house …**
Je déteste ma maison …	I hate my house …
parce qu'il y a …	because there is …
trop de bruit	too much noise
il y a trop de monde	there are too many people
il n'y a pas …	there is not
assez de	enough
place	space

Tu peux décrire ta chambre?	**Can you describe your bedroom?**
Qu'est-ce qu'il y a?	What is there?
As-tu un/une/des … ?	Have you got a/some … ?
Oui, j'ai un/une/des …	Yes, I've got a/some …
Non, je n'ai pas de/d' …	No, I don't have …
Dans ma chambre …	In my bedroom…
il y a …	there is … / there are …
une armoire en bois	a wooden wardrobe
une chaise verte	a green chair
une commode	a chest of drawers
une lampe rose	a pink lamp
une table	a table
des lits superposés	bunk beds
un ordinateur	a computer
des posters	posters
des rideaux rouges	red curtains
des CD	some CDs
une chaîne stéréo	a stereo system
une étagère	a bookcase
dans	in
par terre	on the floor
sous	under
sur	on

Relationships

Tu t'entends bien avec ta famille?	**Do you get on well with your family?**
Je m'entends bien avec mon père/frère mais je ne m'entends pas bien avec ma mère/sœur.	I get on well with my father/ brother but I don't get on well with my mother/sister.
Qui est le membre de ta famille que tu préfères?	Who is your favourite family member?

Je préfère mon père/frère/ ma mère/sœur parce qu'il/ elle est …
I prefer my father/brother/ mother/sister because he/ she is …
amusant(e) — funny
sympa — nice
cool — cool

Tu préfères manger à table ou devant la télé?
Do you prefer to eat at the table or in front of the TV?

Je préfère manger à table. — I prefer to eat at the table.
Je préfère manger devant la télé. — I prefer to eat in front of the TV.
Pourquoi? — Why?
Parce que c'est plus sociable. — It's more sociable.
On peut parler ensemble. — We can talk together.
C'est plus commode. — It's more comfortable.
J'adore regarder la télé. — I love watching TV.

Vous faites quelles sortes de choses ensemble?
What kinds of things do you do together?
Nous … — We …
faisons les courses — go shopping
mangeons — eat
allons en vacances — go on holiday
allons à l'église — go to church
regardons la télé — watch TV
faisons du sport — do sport

Working or studying

Quelle est ta matière préférée?
What's your favourite subject?
Ma matière préférée est … — My favourite subject is …
C'est … — It's …
le sport — PE
le français — French
le dessin — art
la musique — music
la technologie — CDT
l'anglais — English
l'espagnol — Spanish
l'histoire-géo — social subjects
les maths — maths
les sciences — science
l'informatique — computing
les études ménagères — home economics
la religion — RE

HOMEWORK CLUB

Aimes-tu … ?
Do you like … ?
C'est … — It's …
ennuyeux — boring
génial — great
intéressant — interesting
nul — rubbish
super — fantastic
Bof! — It's not bad.
Ça va. — It's OK.

Dans le lycée, il y a …
In the school, there is/are …
une bibliothèque — a library
une cantine — a canteen
des laboratoires — laboratories
un club de judo — a judo club
un club de football — a football club
un club de hockey — a hockey club
un club de devoirs — a homework club
un club d'échecs — a chess club
un club d'art dramatique — a drama club
un orchestre — an orchestra

Mon lycée …
My school …
s'appelle Liberton High School. — is called Liberton High School.
Liberton High School est un lycée mixte. — Liberton High School is a mixed school.
C'est assez grand. — It's quite big.
Il y a environ neuf cent élèves et soixante professeurs. — There are around 900 students and 60 teachers.

Qu'est-ce que tu fair au lycée?
What do you do at school?
Le lycée commence à huit heures vingt-cinq et finit à trois heures vingt-cinq. — School starts at 8.25 and finishes at 3.25.
Il y a une récréation à onze heures moins le quart. — There's a break at 10.45.
La pause de midi est à deux heures moins dix. — Lunch is at 1.50.

On a quatre cours le matin et deux cours l'après-midi.	We have four lessons in the morning and two in the afternoon.	porter des manteaux dans la classe	wear jackets in class
Un cours dure environ cinquante minutes.	One lesson lasts about 50 minutes.	parler au même temps que le prof	speak when the teacher is speaking
On va au lycée tous les jours sauf le week-end.	We go to school every day except the weekend.	bavarder avec les amis dans la classe	chat to friends in class
On a le droit de …	You are allowed to …	utiliser des portables dans la classe	use mobiles in class
On n'a pas le droit de …	You are not allowed to …	écouter de la musique dans la classe	listen to music in class
fumer	smoke	mâcher le chewing-gum	to chew chewing gum
porter des baskets	wear trainers		
porter du maquillage	wear make-up		

Jobs and future employment

Tu as un petit boulot?	**Do you have a part-time job?**	*Je voudrais travailler avec …*	I would like to work with …
		les enfants	children
Oui, je travaille dans un …	Yes, I work in a …	*les personnes âgées*	old people
supermarché	supermarket	*les malades*	ill people
magasin	shop	*les animaux*	animals
		les ordinateurs	computers

Je suis …	**I am …**
Je voudrais être …	I would like to be a/an …
Il / Elle est …	He/She is a/an …
acteur / actrice	actor
agent de police	police officer
fille / garçon au pair	au pair
boucher(–ère)	butcher
boulanger(–ère)	baker
caissier(–ère)	cashier
chauffeur	driver
coiffeur(–euse)	hairdresser
dentiste	dentist
fermier(–ère)	farmer
hôtesse de l'air	air hostess
jardinier(–ère)	gardener
infirmier(–ère)	nurse
médecin	doctor
professeur	teacher
secrétaire	secretary
serveur(–euse)	waiter/waitress
technicien(–ne)	technician
vendeur(–euse)	sales assistant
vétérinaire	vet
au chomage	unemployed
Je voudrais travailler …	I would like to work …
Je ne voudrais pas travailler …	I wouldn't like to work …
dans un magasin	in a shop
dans une usine	in a factory
dans le commerce	in business
dans l'informatique	in computing
dans un bureau	in an office

Pocket money

Est-ce que …	Do you …
tu reçois de l'argent de poche?	receive pocket money?
tu as un petit boulot?	have a part time job?
tu travailles?	work?
Tu reçois combien de l'argent de poche?	How much pocket money do you get?
Je reçois …	I get …
dix livres	ten pounds
par semaine	per week
de mes parents	from my parents
de ma grand-mère	from my grandmother
Je ne reçois pas d'argent de poche.	I don't get pocket money.
Je reçois de l'argent …	I receive money …
quand j'en ai besoin	when I need it
J'ai un petit boulot.	I have a part time job
Je ne pense pas que …	I don't think that …
Mes parents me donnent …	My parents give me …
assez d'argent	enough money

Je travaille …	I work …
dans un supermarché	in a supermarket
dans un bureau	in an office
dans un magasin	in a shop

Household tasks

Qu'est-ce que tu fais …	What do you do …
Pour aider chez toi?	To help at home?
Je fais …	I do …
le ménage	the housework
la vaisselle	the dishes
la lessive	the washing/laundry
le repassage	the ironing
la cuisine	the cooking
les courses	the shopping
Je fais du baby-sitting.	I babysit.
Je range ma chambre.	I tidy my room.
Je nettoie la salle de bains.	I clean the bathroom.
Je passe l'aspirateur.	I do the hovering.
Je lave la voiture.	I wash the car.
Je lave les vitres / fenêtres.	I wash the windows.

Hobbies and sports

Quels sont tes passe-temps?	What are your hobbies?
Qu'est-ce que tu aimes faire?	What do you like to do?
Qu'est-ce que tu n'aimes pas faire?	What do you not like to do?
Mes passe-temps sont …	My hobbies are …
J'aime …	I like …
Je n'aime pas …	I don't like …
jouer au tennis	playing tennis

jouer au football	playing football
faire de la natation	going swimming
lire des livres	reading books
aller à la discothèque	going to clubs
aller au cinéma	going to the cinema
aller aux restaurants	going to restaurants
aller au club de jeunes	going to the youth club
sortir avec mes amis	going out with my friends

Qu'est–ce que tu fais pendant ton temps libre?	What do you do in your free time?
Je joue au tennis.	I play tennis.
Je fais de la natation.	I go swimming.
Je fais du cyclisme.	I go cycling.
Je fais du VTT.	I go mountain-biking.
Je fais de l'équitation.	I go horse-riding.
Je joue au rugby.	I play ruby.
Je fais de la voile.	I go sailing.
Je fais de la planche à voile.	I go windsurfing.
Je vais à la pêche.	I go fishing.
Je lis des livres.	I read books.
Je vais à la discothèque.	I go to clubs.
Je sors avec mes amis.	I go out with my friends.

The weather

Quel temps fait-il?	What's the weather like?		
Il y a du soleil.	It's sunny.	*Il fait du vent.*	It's windy.
Il fait froid.	It's cold.	*Il y a des orages.*	It's stormy.
Il fait chaud.	It's hot.	*dans le nord*	in the north
Il pleut.	It's raining.	*dans le sud*	in the south
Il fait beau.	It's good weather.	*dans l'est*	in the east
Il fait mauvais.	It's bad weather.	*dans l'ouest*	in the west
Il neige.	It's snowing.	*il fera chaud*	it will be hot
Il y a du brouillard.	It's foggy.	*il y aura du brouillard*	it will be foggy

Past holidays

Pendant l'été ...	In the summer ...	J'ai voyagé en ...	I travelled by ...
L'année dernière ...	Last year ...	*train*	train
La semaine dernière ...	Last week ...	*avion*	plane
Le mois dernier	Last month ...	*bus*	bus
je suis allé(e) en Espagne	I went to Spain	*voiture*	car
je suis allé(e) à Paris	I went to Paris		

Pour ...	For ...	Qu'est-ce que tu as fait?	What did you do?
Je suis resté(e) là pour ...	I stayed there for ...	*Je me suis fait bronzé(e).*	I sunbathed.
quinze jours	a fortnight	*Je suis allé(e) à la plage / piscine.*	I went to the beach/ swimming pool.
une semaine	one week	*J'ai fait des achats.*	I went shopping.
deux semaines	two weeks	*J'ai fait une promenade.*	I went for a walk.
trois semaines	three weeks	*Nous sommes allé(e)s à la discothèque.*	We went to the nightclub.

Je suis allé(e) avec...	I went with ...		
ma famille	my family	*Nous avons mangé dans un restaurant.*	We ate in a restaurant.
mes amis	my friends	*Nous sommes allé(e)s au cinéma.*	We went to the cinema.
ma grand-mère	my grandmother	*Nous avons fait de la planche à voile.*	We went windsurfing.

J'ai logé dans ...	I stayed in ...		
un hôtel	a hotel		
un appartement	a flat, an apartment	C'était ...	It was ...
une caravane	a caravan	*super!*	fantastic!
une auberge de jeunesse	a youth hostel	*chouette!*	great!
un gîte	a cottage	*amusant!*	fun!
une chambre d'hôte	a B&B	*ennuyeux!*	boring!

nul!	rubbish!
Il faisait du soleil.	It was sunny.
Il pleuvait.	It was raining.
Il y avait du vent.	It was windy.

La nourriture était …	**The food was …**
dégoûtante	disgusting
bonne	good
moche	rubbish

Les gens étaient …	**The people were …**
sympas	nice
aimables	friendly
serviables	helpful
impolis	impolite
désagréables	unpleasant

Future holidays

L'année prochaine …	Next year …
Quand je serai plus grand(e)	When I'm older
j'irai en/à …	I'll go to …
Je vais aller en/à …	I am going to …
Je voudrais aller en/à …	I would like to go to …
parce que c'est	because it's …
parce qu'il y a	because there is/are …
beaucoup à faire	lots to do
des musées intéressants	interesting museums
de grandes discothèques	big nightclubs
de belles plages	beautiful beaches
Je ferai des achats	I will go shopping
Je ferais des achats	I would go shopping
J'achèterai …	I will buy …
J'achèterais …	I would buy …
Je visiterai tous les monuments historiques.	I will visit all the historical monuments.
Je visiterais …	I would visit …
Je me ferai bronzer.	I will sunbathe.
Je me ferais bronzer.	I would sunbathe.

Health

le corps	**the body**	*J'ai les cheveux …*	I have … hair
la tête	head	*gras*	greasy
la bouche	mouth	*secs*	dry
les cheveux	hair	*beaux*	beautiful
la dent (les dents)	tooth (teeth)	*le bras (les bras)*	arm(s)
la lèvre (les lèvres)	lip(s)	*le cou*	neck
le nez	nose	*le doigt (les doigts)*	finger(s)
l'oreille (les oreilles)	ear(s)	*le dos*	back
un œil (les yeux)	eye(s)	*l'épaule (les épaules)*	shoulder(s)
la peau	skin	*le genou (les genoux)*	knee(s)
le sourcil (les sourcils)	eyebrow(s)	*la jambe (les jambes)*	leg(s)

la main (les mains)	hand(s)
le pied (les pieds)	foot (feet)
la langue	tongue
J'ai mal.	I'm not well.
J'ai …	I have …
mal aux oreilles	earache
mal aux dents	toothache
mal à la tête	a headache
mal aux pieds	sore feet
mal au ventre	stomach ache
mal à la gorge	a sore throat
de la fièvre	a temperature
J'ai chaud.	I'm hot.
J'ai froid.	I'm cold.
Je tousse.	I've got a cough.

Vous devriez … — You should …

prendre de l'aspirine.	take some aspirine.
prendre du sirop.	take some cough mixture.
rester au lit/au chaud.	stay in bed/in the warmth.
sucer des pastilles pour la gorge.	suck throat pastilles.
mettre un pull.	put on a jumper
aller chez le dentiste.	go to the dentist.

Vous désirez — What would you like?

Je voudrais quelque chose pour …	I would like something for …
Voici …	Here is/are …
des comprimés	some pills
de l'aspirine	some aspirin
du sirop	some cough mixture
des mouchoirs en papier	some paper tissues

Il faut … — You should …

manger cinq portions de fruit et légumes chaque jour.	eat five portions of fruit and vegetables each day.
Il faut boire huit verres d'eau chaque jour.	You should drink eight glasses of water each day.
Pour être en forme, c'est nécessaire de faire trente minutes d'exercice trois fois par semaine.	To keep fit, it's necessary to do 30 minutes' exercise three times a week.
Fumer et boire d'alcool est mauvais pour la santé.	Smoking and drinking alcohol is bad for your health.

Je suis … — I'm …

en bonne forme.	fit and healthy.
Je ne suis pas en bonne forme.	I'm not fit and healthy.
Je suis en mauvaise forme.	I'm in bad shape.

Je mène une vie saine.	I lead a healthy lifestyle.
Je joue au …	I play …
trois fois par semaine	three times a week
Je mange beaucoup de …	I eat (lots of)
Je bois …	I drink …
Je suis dépendant(e) de …	I'm addicted to …

Je devrais … — I should …

faire plus d'exercice.	do more exercise.
manger plus sainement.	eat more healthily.
boire plus d'eau.	drink more water.

Smoking, alcohol and drugs

le tabac	smoking
l'alcool	alcohol
la drogue	drugs
Le tabac est mauvais pour les poumons.	Smoking is bad for the lungs.
On peut devenir accros à la drogue.	You can become addicted to drugs.
On ne peut pas s'arrêter.	You can't stop.
Je suis pour/contre …	I'm for/against …
C'est cool.	It's cool.
C'est reposant.	It's relaxing.
On a plus de confiance.	You are more confident.
On a l'air plus adulte.	You seem more grown up.
Je m'amuse sans fumer.	I enjoy myself without smoking.
Les cigarettes coûtent chers.	Cigarettes are expensive.

The environment

la belle terre	the beautiful world/earth
le ciel	the sky
les arcs-en-ciel	rainbows
l'air	the air
la lumière	light
le jour	the day
la nuit	the night
l'eau	water
les cascades	waterfalls
les rivières	rivers
la mer	the sea
les océans	oceans
les vagues	waves
les poissons	fish
les champs	fields
les collines	hills
les montagnes	mountains
les enfants	children
les animaux	animals
les oiseaux	birds
les fleurs	flowers
les plantes	plants
les fôrets	forests
les arbres	trees
les fruits	fruits
les jardins	gardens
les planètes	planets
le soleil	sun
la lune	moon

les étoiles	stars
les nuages	clouds
le silence	silence
le bruit	noise
L'environnement, c'est important.	The environment is important.
On doit …	One must …
protéger …	protect
la terre	the earth
sauver les animaux en danger	save endangered animals
sauver les dauphins	save the dolphins
sauver les baleines	save the whales
protéger les fôrets tropicales	protect the rainforests

Meals and food

Qu'est-ce que tu manges ... ?	What do you eat ... ?
pour ...	for ...
le petit déjeuner	breakfast
le déjeuner	lunch
le dîner	dinner
Je mange ...	I eat ...
du pain	bread
du beurre	butter
des céréales	cereal
de la confiture	jam
du pain grillé	toast

Tu aimes manger ... ?	Do you like eating ... ?
les légumes	vegetables
la viande	meat
J'aime beaucoup manger ...	I really like eating ...
Je déteste absolument manger ...	I absolutely hate eating ...
le chou	cabbage
le chou-fleur	cauliflower
la salade verte	lettuce
les haricots verts	green beens
les petits pois	peas
les tomates	tomatoes
les pommes de terre	potatoes
les frites	chips
le bifteck	steak
le bœuf	beef
le jambon	ham
le poulet	chicken
le saucisson	sausage

Quel est ton dessert préféré?	What is your favourite dessert?
comme dessert	as a dessert
Je préfère manger ...	I prefer to eat ...
du fromage frais	soft white cheese
du yaourt	yoghurt
du gâteau	cake
de la glace	ice cream
de la mousse au chocolat	chocolate mousse
des fruits	fruit
des abricots	apricots
des bananes	bananas
des fraises	strawberries
des framboises	rasperries
des mûres	blackberries
des oranges	oranges
des pêches	peaches
des poires	pears
des pommes	apples
des prunes	plums

Comme snack je mange ...	For a snack I eat ...
des chips	crisps
du chocolat	chocolate
du fromage	cheese
un sandwich	a sandwich
un steak-frites	steak and chips
un croissant	a croissant
un pain au chocolat	a croissant with chocolate inside
une baguette	a stick of French bread

Qu'est-ce que tu bois?	What do you drink?
Je bois ...	I drink ...
une boisson chaude	a hot drink
une boisson froide	a cold drink
du thé	tea
du café	coffee
du café au lait	white coffee
du chocolat (chaud)	(hot) chocolate
de l'eau	water
de l'eau minérale	mineral water
du jus d'orange	orange juice
du lait	milk
de la limonade	lemonade

Vous voulez combien?

How much would you like?

Je voudrais …
un kilo de bananes
un litre de lait
un morceau de gâteau
un paquet de chips
un panier de fraises
une livre de pommes
une bouteille de bière
une boîte de champignons

I would like …
a kilo of bananas
a litre of milk
a piece of cake
a packet of crisps
a basket of strawberries
a pound of apples
a bottle of beer
a box of mushrooms

une portion de frites
une tranche de jambon
100 grammes de sucre

a portion of chips
a slice of ham
100 grams of sugar

Vous désirez?
Je voudrais …
C'est combien?
L'addition s'il vous plaît.
Ça fait …
dix euros vingt cinq

What would you like?
I would like …
How much is it?
The bill, please.
That's …
10 euros 25

Transcripts

The audio files which accompany the General and Credit paper Listening exam questions reproduced in this book can be found online at: www.brightredpublishing.co.uk

The text for these recordings is printed below.

Look out for

To make sure that you are getting the most benefit from this book, only refer to these transcripts after you have attempted the examples in Chapter 4, The Listening Paper. That way, you simulate exam conditions. Remember that you will not be able to read the French text for the recordings in the exam.

 The self-test icons show that this audio file accompanies one of the questions you worked through on your own and answers for these questions are printed at the end of the book.

Complete the sentences in English

Example 1 (2004 General Listening Q2)

Audio file 01

Demain on va passer la journée en ville.

Audio file 02

Tu sais, le samedi matin, il y a un marché sur la place.

Audio file 03

L'après-midi, on va au centre sportif voir mes copains.

Example 2 (2005 General Listening Q7)

🎧 **Audio file 04**

Moi, j'adore l'Écosse. J'ai visité l'<u>Écosse</u> pour la première fois en dix-neuf cent quatre-vingt-dix.

🎧 **Audio file 05**

On a fait un <u>échange de maisons</u> avec une famille écossaise car nous n'avions pas beaucoup d'argent.

🎧 **Audio file 06**

Je <u>retourne en Écosse</u> tous les deux ans pour les matchs de rugby et aussi pour les vacances.

Example 3 (2003 General Listening Q4)

🎧 **Audio file 07**

Je travaille le week-end et le jeudi soir dans un petit supermarché. C'est assez intéressant. Je remplis les rayons, j'aide les clients à trouver les articles qu'ils cherchent et, ce que j'aime le plus, je travaille à la caisse.

Example 4 (2007 General Listening Q13)

🎧 **Audio file 08**

L'équipe d'animation invite les adolescents à un repas spécial ce soir à 20h30. Venez faire la connaissance d'autres jeunes dans le camping et découvrez les activités organisées pour vous.

True or False

Example 1 (2005 General Listening Q10)

🎧 **Audio file 09**

Il faut visiter le château de Chambord qui est situé dans une grande forêt. C'est le plus grand château de la région et on dit qu'il y a une cheminée pour chaque jour de l'année.

Example 2 (2004 General Listening Q7)

🎧 **Audio file 10**

C'est un stade très moderne, près de la ville. Il y a des places pour trente mille spectateurs et un parking énorme derrière le stade.

Example 3 (2003 General Listening Q9)

🎧 **Audio file 11**

*Dans dix jours, je pars en vacances en Finlande avec mes parents - pour six semaines!
On va loger chez mon oncle et ma tante qui habitent là-bas. Ce sera formidable!*

Tick the box

Example 1 (2005 General Listening Q2)

🎧 **Audio file 12**

Pont-Saint-Martin c'est un petit village tout près de Nantes. Dans le village il y a une petite église, la mairie et plusieurs magasins.

Example 2 (2006 General Listening Q2)

🎧 **Audio file 13**

Le camping n'est pas très grand et c'est vraiment tranquille ici. Il y a beaucoup à faire pour les enfants, par exemple il y a une piscine en plein air et une salle de jeux.

Example 3 (2003 General Listening Q7)

🎧 **Audio file 14**

Salut! Je m'appelle Jean-Claude. Bienvenue en France! Quand es-tu arrivé? Combien de temps vas-tu rester ici? Tu as déjà visité cette région de la France?

Fill in the boxes

Example 1 (2006 General Listening Q5)

🎧 **Audio file 15**

Ma femme et moi, nous travaillons à plein temps et nous n'avons pas beaucoup de temps pour nous relaxer. Moi, je travaille dans une boulangerie et je dois me lever tôt le matin. Ma femme est infirmière et de temps en temps elle doit travailler jusqu'à dix heures du soir.

Example 2 (2006 General Listening Q8)

🎧 **Audio file 16**

À la maison, c'est moi qui sors la poubelle et c'est ma sœur Mireille qui met la table. Mais ici au camping, je fais la vaisselle et Mireille achète le pain le matin.

Mention one thing

Example 1 (2005 General Listening Q1)

🎧 **Audio file 17**

Tu veux quelque chose à manger?

Example 2 (2003 Credit Listening Q4)

🎧 **Audio file 18**

Parfois, mes parents s'inquiètent pour moi. À part mes amis au lycée, j'ai peu de contact avec des gens de mon âge; donc, mes parents ont organisé un échange.

Example 3 (2006 Credit Listening Q1)

🎧 **Audio file 19**

Voici ma sœur, Nicole. Nous sommes jumeaux. Heureusement, nous nous entendons très bien. J'ai de très bons rapports avec elle.

Mention a number of things

Example 1 (2007 Credit Listening Qs9, 10)

🎧 **Audio file 20**

Ça fait trois ans que j'habite en Écosse et je viens d'acheter une nouvelle maison sur la côte ouest. Ma femme et moi, nous avons de très bons amis là-bas.

🎧 **Audio file 21**

Au début, je ne connaissais personne. Et, en plus, j'avais du mal à comprendre les Écossais à cause de leur accent.

Example 2 (2006 Credit Listening Qs2–4)

🎧 **Audio file 22**

En général, on passe seulement une semaine ici en juillet parce que mon mari doit travailler. Pour nous, les vacances principales sont en hiver. Nous passons une quinzaine à faire du ski en Suisse.

🎧 **Audio file 23**

Passer les vacances ici, ça me plaît beaucoup. Il y a tant de choses à faire pour les jeunes. Il y a un parc d'attractions pas loin d'ici. Et en plus, on peut faire de l'équitation.

🎧 **Audio file 24**

Moi, j'ai la chance d'être doué pour le sport. Je fais des sports d'équipe et des sports individuels. Au collège, je suis champion de natation.

Answers

 You can check your answers to the self-test questions in Chapter 2 Dictionary Skills, Chapter 3 The Reading Paper and Chapter 4 The Listening Paper below. Here's hoping you did well!

Chapter 2 Dictionary skills

Verbs

Question 1

1 a) *voir* b) to see c) he sees

2 a) *habiter* b) to live c) she lives

3 a) *essayer* b) to try c) you try

4 a) *s'inscrire* b) to apply/register c) I apply/register

5 a) *s'habiller* b) to get dressed c) we get dressed

6 a) *être* b) to be c) they are

7 a) *faire* b) to do/make c) they (fem.) do/make

8 a) *recevoir* b) to receive c) you receive

Words that have more than one meaning

Question 1

1 b) book; **2** a) spend; **3** b) map; **4** a) shut; **5** b) bed; **6** b) language; **7** a) run; **8** b) wears.

Question 2

1 a) leaf, sheet b) sheet; **2** a) make, do, b) make

Looking up longer words and phrases

Example 1

The man, who was paying no attention to the road, because he was on his phone, crashed into the barrier and dented it.

Example 2

I am very worried at the thought of failing all my exams in spite of my efforts to study regularly.

Example 3

Her father should support her with her dream of becoming a professional singer but, on the contrary, he insists that she study law at university.

Chapter 3 The Reading paper

Complete the sentences in English

Example 2 (2005 General Reading Q6)

1 … fish and meat.

2 … menu.

3 … the accounts.

4 … several towns.

5 … opened his own restaurant.

Example 3 (2006 General Reading Q4)

1 … leave their houses.

2 … constant rain.

3 … disappeared.

4 … have lost their houses.

Example 4 (2006 General Reading Q7)

(a) … already been abroad.

(b) … the most popular destinations.

(c) … getting to know other people.

Example 5 (2007 General Reading Q2)

1 … on holiday by the sea.

2 … he liked her.

3 … thinks about her all the time.

Tick True or False

Example 2 (2005 General Reading Q10)

1 True

2 False (She went with a friend and her teacher saw her there.)

3 True

Tick the box

Example 2 (2006 General Reading Q2)

1 Tons of sand have been brought to the river Seine.

2 There are also seats, parasols and palm trees.

3 At night there will be shows and dinners.

Write down someone's name

Example 2 (2007 General Reading Q3)

1 Gerald.

2 Emeline.

3 Noël.

4 Emeline.

Mention one thing

Example 2 (2004 Credit Reading Q6)

(d) They have adopted a code of conduct and no longer employ children.

(e) The children's families, who were dependent on their earning money, may die of hunger.

Mention a number of things

Example 3 (2007 Credit Reading Q4)

To go and live in a more developed country.

To find work and a better standard of living.

Example 4 (2005 Credit Reading Q4)

He sold double-glazed windows.

His sister's nephew found him the job.

Example 5 (2004 Credit Reading Q3)

A motorway and a high speed train.

Chapter 4 The Listening Paper

Complete the sentences in English

Example 3 (2003 General Listening Q4)

1 supermarket

2 find the products they need

3 works at the checkout.

Example 4 (2007 General Listening Q13)

1 a meal, dinner

2 other young people

3 the activities available.

Tick True or False

Example 2 (2004 General Listening Q7)

1 False (It's near the town, not in the town.)

2 False (The stadium holds 30,000 spectators, not 50,000.)

3 True

Example 3 (2003 General Listening Q9)

1 False (He is leaving in ten days.)

2 True

3 False (His aunt and uncle live there.)

Tick the box

Example 2 (2006 General Listening Q2)

It's really quiet.

There is a lot for the children to do.

There is a swimming pool.

Example 3 (2003 General Listening Q7)

When did you arrive?

How long are you here for?

Have you been to this part of France before?

Fill in the boxes

Example 2 (2006 General Listening Q8)

(Antoine's job at home) Puts out the rubbish bin; (at the campsite) Does the dishes

(Mireille's job at home) Sets the table; (at the campsite) Buys the bread in the morning

Mention one thing

Example 3 (2006 Credit Listening Q1)

I have a (very) good relationship with her. I get on well with her.

Mention a number of things

Example 2 (2006 Credit Listening Qs2–4)

Two of the following points:

There is lots for young people to do.

There is a theme park near by.

You can go horseriding.

Any two of the following points:

He's good at sport.

He does team and individual sports.

At school he's a swimming champion.